Green, Gold & Glorious

THE GREEN BAY PACKERS' MAGICAL RUN TO SUPER BOWL XLV

Presented by

GREEN BAY PRESS-GAZETTE
greenbaypressgazette.com

Published by Pediment Publishing, a division of The Pediment Group, Inc. www.pediment.com Printed in Canada.

Foreword

When it comes to the 2010 Green Bay Packers, remember one thing. They did it the hard way. Quarterback Aaron Rodgers raised the stakes even before the season, dressing for Texas – and Super Bowl XLV – at the team's annual welcome luncheon.

The Packers were a popular preseason pick for the Super Bowl, and then staggered to a 3-3 start.

Sixteen players landed on the injured reserve list, including six starters.

All six regular-season losses came by four or fewer points, including two in overtime.

Rodgers sustained two concussions and missed 1½ games.

Such adversity would have doomed most teams. But the Packers still were alive in late December, still doing it the hard way.

They needed to win their final two regular-season games at Lambeau Field to make the playoffs.

They crushed the New York Giants 45-17 and followed up with a 10-3 win over their old archrivals, the Chicago Bears. That gave them a 10-6 record and the final NFC playoff berth.

The Packers then accomplished what no sixth-seeded NFC team had ever done, winning three consecutive postseason road games to punch their ticket to the Super Bowl.

That rugged path included victories at Philadelphia and at Atlanta that were sparked by six Rodgers touchdown passes and three Tramon Williams interceptions.

In a classic NFC championship game at Soldier Field in Chicago, the Packers defeated the Bears thanks in large part to a pair of interceptions by rookie Sam Shields and another by nose tackle B.J. Raji that was returned for a touchdown in the fourth quarter.

No matter what was thrown at the Packers during the 2010 season, they never wavered in their quest to earn a Super Bowl berth.

That drive took the Packers to their fifth Super Bowl, where they defeated the Pittsburgh Steelers for their 13th NFL championship. No team has more titles. ■

RIGHT: Quarterback Aaron Rodgers teased fans with the promise of going to Dallas for Super Bowl XLV when he wore a cowboy hat, bolo tie and duster to the Green Bay Area Chamber of Commerce's annual Welcome Packers luncheon at the Lambeau Field Atrium on Sept. 1. He was escorted to his seat by chamber ambassador Sue May. He supplied cowboy hats to some of his teammates, according to those at his table. Coach Mike McCarthy saw that and said "I see a number of players are already dressed for Dallas, Texas." M.P. KING/GREEN BAY PRESS-GAZETTE

Table of Contents

Philadelphia Eagles

September 12, 2010 • Lincoln Financial Field, Philadelphia • W 27-20

P HILADELPHIA — The Green Bay Packers almost lived a Michael Vick nightmare.
Playing in the second half for injured Kevin Kolb, Vick showed he still had the legs to scare the bejesus out of a defense.

His efforts to rally the Philadelphia Eagles from a 17-point deficit fell short because the Packers made just enough plays against his scattershot throwing and stopped him on a critical fourth-and-1 run in the game's final minutes.

With Kolb out with a concussion, Vick ran for 103 yards – the most by any opposing quarterback in Packers history – on a variety of scrambles, draws and straight runs; threw for 175 yards with a 101.9 passer rating on mostly short throws; and put up 17 points in the game's final 20 minutes.

The Packers won because they made a stop on Vick when they absolutely had to in the game's final minutes. On fourth-and-1 with 2 minutes left, Vick ran straight into the line out of the shotgun. The Packers were ready, and linebackers Clay Matthews, Nick Barnett and Brad Jones stuffed him for no gain, in effect ending the game because the Eagles were out of time outs.

Aaron Rodgers threw two interceptions, but also had a big 32-yard touchdown pass to receiver Greg Jennings. Backup halfbacks Brandon Jackson and John Kuhn combined for a respectable 69 yards rushing on 16 carries in the second half to control some clock and give the Packers the win.

The Packers lost halfback Ryan Grant for the season with an ankle injury after he'd carried only eight times. ∎

OPPOSITE: Running back Ryan Grant (25) is brought down by Eagles defensive tackle Broderick Bunkley (97), linebacker Akeem Jordan (56) and safety Quintin Mikell (27). EVAN SIEGLE/PRESS-GAZETTE

RIGHT: Linebacker Clay Matthews sacks Eagles quarterback Kevin Kolb. Kolb sustained a concussion later in the game and was replaced by Michael Vick.

EVAN SIEGLE/PRESS-GAZETTE

PACKERS**FINAL**

G **27** Eagles **20** » Packers close door in opener

NEAR VICKTIMS

Green Bay Packers linebackers Clay Matthews (52), Brad Jones (49) and Nick Barnett (56) converge on Philadelphia Eagles quarterback Michael Vick on a fourth-and-1 play near the end of the fourth quarter of Sunday's game at Lincoln Financial Field in Philadelphia. Safety Nick Collins (36) is at left. **Photos by Evan Siegle/Press-Gazette**

Defense stuffs QB on critical fourth-and-1 to stop comeback

BY PETE DOUGHERTY
pdougherty@greenbaypressgazette.com

PHILADELPHIA — The Green Bay Packers almost lived a Michael Vick nightmare on Sunday.

Vick still might not be the quarterback he was before going to prison in 2007 for his role in a dog-fighting ring, but while playing in the second half for injured Kevin Kolb, he showed he still has the legs to scare the bejesus out of a defense.

His efforts to rally the Philadelphia Eagles from a 17-point deficit fell short because the Packers made just enough

McCarthy said after the game.

It also was a different opponent than McCarthy expected to face. When the Packers began game planning for this matchup in the offseason, the Eagles had traded Donovan McNabb so they could turn over their offense to Kolb, a fourth-year pro. But Kolb flopped in his first half as the team's new franchise quarterback, putting up only three points, 49 total yards and a measly 56.2 passer rating in the first two quarters. He looked much inferior to Packers quarterback Aaron Rodgers even though Rodgers was hardly on top of his game.

Maybe Kolb would have bounced

rating on mostly short throws; and put up 17 points in the game's final 20 minutes. But the Packers didn't let him make the difference in the game, either. They sacked him three times in the fourth quarter — once each by Frank Zombo, Cullen Jenkins and Clay Matthews — and didn't give up any deep throws (Vick's longest completion was for 27 yards).

Afterward, the sense of relief that they'd weathered Vick was palpable.

"You expect Vick to get in there, but you don't expect him to be the quarterback the second half every snap," defensive end Ryan Pickett said. "He brings so many different dimensions to the game. It's hard to stop the run

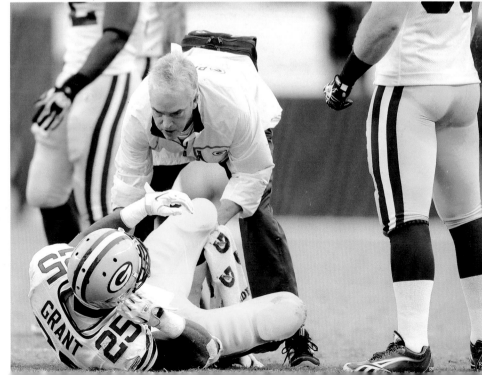

ABOVE: Running back Ryan Grant (25) breaks away from Eagles defensive tackle Broderick Bunkley (97) and linebacker Trent Cole (58) during the second quarter. Grant sustained a season-ending ankle injury on the play. EVAN SIEGLE/PRESS-GAZETTE

ABOVE RIGHT: Grant falls to the ground at the end of the run. EVAN SIEGLE/PRESS-GAZETTE

RIGHT: Grant is assisted by Packers trainer Pepper Burruss after getting hurt on the play.
EVAN SIEGLE/PRESS-GAZETTE

RIGHT: Linebacker Nick Barnett (56) pressures Eagles quarterback Michael Vick (7). EVAN SIEGLE/PRESS-GAZETTE

FAR RIGHT: From left, safety Nick Collins (36) and linebackers Clay Matthews (52), Brad Jones (49) and Nick Barnett (56) stop Eagles quarterback Michael Vick (7) on fourth-and-1 in near the end of the fourth quarter. EVAN SIEGLE/PRESS-GAZETTE

BOTTOM: Defensive end Justin Harrell (91) pressures Eagles quarterback Michael Vick (7). Harrell sustained a season-ending knee injury later in the game. EVAN SIEGLE/PRESS-GAZETTE

OPPOSITE: Linebacker Clay Matthews (52) signals for a first down after the Packers stuffed Eagles quarterback Michael Vick (7) on fourth down in the fourth quarter. EVAN SIEGLE/PRESS-GAZETTE

Buffalo Bills

September 19, 2010 • Lambeau Field, Green Bay • W 34-7

Conservative play calling and quarterback play can take an undermanned team only so far in the NFL. In the Buffalo Bills' case, it kept them relatively competitive with the Green Bay Packers for one half. But that was about it in the regular-season opener at Lambeau Field, where the Packers' huge advantages at quarterback, receiver and pass rush made this game as stark a mismatch as the final score suggested.

The Packers looked to have the makings of a Super Bowl contender while the Bills were starting over with a new coach in Chan Gailey and one of the least talented rosters in the league.

The differences started at quarterback, where the enormous gap in arm strength and athleticism between Aaron Rodgers and the Bills' Trent Edwards was enough to determine the outcome.

Rodgers also had an array of talent to throw to in tight end Jermichael Finley (four catches for 103 yards) and receivers Donald Driver, Greg Jennings, James Jones and Jordy Nelson (12 catches combined). Edwards had only one playmaker in the passing game, receiver Lee Evans, and was unable to complete even a single pass to him.

Edwards barely broke the 100-yard mark in passing yards (he had 102), finished with a rotten passer rating (37.0), and threw second-half interceptions to linebacker Brandon Chillar and rookie safety Morgan Burnett that sent the Packers on their way to the blowout.

Packers outside linebacker Clay Matthews continued his dominance through the first two weeks with back-to-back three-sack games. ■

OPPOSITE: Fullback Quinn Johnson stiff-arms Bills linebacker Keith Ellison on an 11-yard pass reception. JIM MATTHEWS/PRESS-GAZETTE

PACKERS**FINAL**

G 34   **Bills** 7   » 2-0: No contest at Lambeau

2ND-HALF SACKING

Green Bay Packers outside linebacker Clay Matthews sacks Buffalo Bills quarterback Trent Edwards in the third quarter during Sunday's home opener at Lambeau Field. Matthews finished with three sacks for the second straight week. **Corey Wilson/Press-Gazette**

Packers' superior talent keeps pressure on Bills until they break

BY PETE DOUGHERTY
pdougher@greenbaypressgazette.com

Conservative play calling and quarterback play can take an undermanned team only so far in the NFL.

In the Buffalo Bills' case, it kept them relatively competitive with the Green Bay Packers for one half Sunday. But that was about it in the regu-

advantages at quarterback, receiver and pass rush made this game as stark a mismatch as the Packers' 34-7 blowout win suggests.

"That's what we need to do to teams, we need to overwhelm them," defensive end Ryan Pickett said.

"They come out fighting hard, but you just keep the pressure on them and eventu-
ally they'll break. I felt like we

pressure on them all game, and in the end our talent and plays and players took over."

The win sets up a big earlyseason matchup next week between the NFC North Division's two leaders, the Packers at the Bears. Both have opened the season 2-0 — the Bears won at Dallas on Sunday — and have jumped two games ahead of 0-2 Minnesota.

Sunday's game probably
about the Packers, considering the status of the two franchises. The Packers, in their fifth season in coach Mike McCarthy's program, have the makings of a Super Bowl contender whereas the Bills are starting over with a new coach in Chan Gailey and one of the least talented rosters in the league.

The differences start at quarterback, where the

strength and athleticism between Aaron Rodgers and the Bills' Trent Edwards was enough to determine the outcome.

➤ See Packers, Page 8

ABOVE: Wide receiver James Jones looks for a place to do a Lambeau Leap after catching a 30-yard touchdown pass from Aaron Rodgers early in the fourth quarter. COREY WILSON/PRESS-GAZETTE

LEFT: These fans came all the way from Spain to watch the Packers. JIM MATTHEWS/PRESS-GAZETTE

FAR LEFT: Quarterback Aaron Rodgers scrambles for a first down. JIM MATTHEWS/PRESS-GAZETTE

OPPOSITE TOP: Wide receiver Donald Driver catches a pass in front of Bills cornerback Drayton Florence. JIM MATTHEWS/PRESS-GAZETTE

OPPOSITE BOTTOM: Fans enjoyed a sunny, mild afternoon as the Packers opened at home against the Bills. JIM MATTHEWS/PRESS-GAZETTE

Chicago Bears

September 27, 2010 • Soldier Field, Chicago • L 20-17

CHICAGO – The Green Bay Packers moved the ball, pressured the quarterback and generally outplayed the Chicago Bears in the teams' first encounter.

But that wasn't enough to stop the Bears from landing the first big blow of the 2010 race for the NFC North Division title.

In a game that brought back memories of the 2006 Chicago team that won the division title and went to the Super Bowl, the Packers were done in by a barrage of penalties and two huge special-teams plays by Bears playmakers.

That set up a climactic final few minutes that saw Bears linebacker Brian Urlacher force the game-turning fumble and kicker Robbie Gould hit a 19-yard field goal with 4 seconds left that gave Chicago the win.

The Packers in many ways got the better of the Bears, outgaining Chicago in total yards, 379-276, using mostly a short, spread passing game.

Quarterback Aaron Rodgers outplayed his counterpart, Jay Cutler, and had the better passer rating (92.5 points to 82.5 points), more completions (34 to 16) and more passing yards (316 to 221).

The Packers also sacked Cutler three times. The Bears never sacked Rodgers.

However, Chicago countered with two winning plays on special teams, a blocked field goal by 6-foot-7 defensive end Julius Peppers in the third quarter and a 62-yard punt return for a touchdown by Devin Hester in the fourth quarter.

Green Bay finished with a team-record 18 penalties. The old record was 17, during a 38-14 victory over the Boston Yanks at State Fair Park in Milwaukee on Oct. 21, 1945. ∎

OPPOSITE: Linebacker A.J. Hawk (50) is leveled by the Bears' Devin Hester (23) during a kickoff return by the Bears' Johnny Knox (13). EVAN SIEGLE/PRESS-GAZETTE

ABOVE: Linebacker Frank Zombo tries to tackle Bears running back Matt Forte (22). COREY WILSON/PRESS-GAZETTE

LEFT: Wide receiver Greg Jennings collides with Bears safety Danieal Manning while trying to make a catch. There was no penalty on the play. EVAN SIEGLE/PRESS-GAZETTE

RIGHT: The Bears' Devin Hester points to the sky before a punt return. EVAN SIEGLE/PRESS-GAZETTE

OPPOSITE TOP LEFT: Tight end Jermichael Finley fights for extra yards after making a catch. EVAN SIEGLE/PRESS-GAZETTE

OPPOSITE TOP RIGHT: Quarterback Aaron Rodgers (12) gestures in the direction of Bears defensive end Julius Peppers (90). EVAN SIEGLE/PRESS-GAZETTE

OPPOSITE BOTTOM: Kicker Mason Crosby (2) watches his 37-yard field goal try during the third quarter. It was blocked by the Bears. EVAN SIEGLE/PRESS-GAZETTE

9.28.10 ★
WWW.PACKERSNEWS.COM
GREEN BAY PRESS-GAZETTE

PACKERS FINAL

© 20 🅖 17 » 3-0 Bears take NFC North lead

MONDAY MISCUES

Chicago Bears linebacker Brian Urlacher, right, knocks the ball out of the hands of Green Bay Packers receiver James Jones in the fourth quarter at Soldier Field in Chicago. Bears cornerback Tim Jennings recovered at the Packers' 46-yard line with 2:18 left. **Evan Siegle/Press-Gazette**

Penalties, special teams gaffes hand Bears victory in showdown

BY PETE DOUGHERTY
jdougherty@greenbaypressgazette.com

CHICAGO — The Green Bay Packers moved the ball, pressured the quarterback and generally outplayed the Chicago Bears for much of Monday night.

But that wasn't enough to stop the Bears from landing the first big blow in the 2010 race for the NFC North Division title.

In a game that brought back memories of the 2006 Chicago team that won the division title and went to the Super Bowl, the Packers were done in by a gave Chicago a 20-17 win at Soldier Field.

"Penalties, special teams, didn't take advantage of our opportunities," Packers safety Nick Collins said. "When you're in a game like this and let the other team hang around, anything is liable to happen."

The win gives the Bears an early jump in the division race, though the season isn't even a quarter old. At 3-0, the Bears have guaranteed themselves at least a split in their season series with the Packers, who are 2-1. Minnesota is in third place at 1-2.

The Packers in many ways got the completions (34 to 16) and more passing yards (316 to 221). The Packers also sacked Cutler three times, whereas the Bears never sacked Rodgers.

However, Chicago countered with two winning plays on special teams, a blocked field goal by 6-foot-7 defensive end Julius Peppers in the third quarter and a 62-yard punt return for a touchdown by Devin Hester, who was the toast of the '06 Bears as a rookie return man, in the fourth quarter.

The Packers also lost two interceptions to penalties that might have been the difference in the fourth quarter. On the first, rookie outside linebacker set up the Bears for their game-winning field goal inside the Packers' 10.

"When you're playing in a close, hard-sought game, you can't negate drive-stopping plays like that with penalties," said Dom Capers, the Packers' defensive coordinator.

The Packers finished with 18 penalties, an ignominious accomplishment that topped the previous team record of 17 set in 1945.

"(Eighteen) penalties, that doesn't cut it," coach Mike McCarthy said. "You can't win football (games) like that."

» See Packers, Page 6

Detroit Lions

October 3, 2010 • Lambeau Field, Green Bay • W 28-26

A quarter of the way through the 2010 schedule, the Green Bay Packers were hardly blowing off anybody's doors.

Despite being a 14½-point favorite, the Packers had to hold off the winless Detroit Lions in the final 6½ minutes for a tense win at Lambeau Field.

Green Bay didn't look like a champion through four games and were nothing like the offensive juggernaut their talent suggested, even while handing the Lions their 23rd straight road loss.

The Packers watched Lions backup quarterback Shaun Hill, starting in place of injured Matthew Stafford, throw for 331 yards and coax defensive coordinator Dom Capers to back off his zone-blitz repertoire. Hill did that by gashing blitzes with several hot reads and screens to convert long third downs.

That said, Capers' unit helped save the win by keeping Detroit out of the end zone in the second half, leaving the Lions with only four Jason Hanson field goals in their comeback from a 28-14 deficit.

The Packers had their chances to win this game convincingly but didn't have the offensive punch (261 yards in total offense) or care with the ball to put the game away. In the second half, Jordy Nelson had a crucial fumble on a kickoff return, and quarterback Aaron Rodgers had two passes to receiver Greg Jennings intercepted.

A surprisingly inert day on which the Packers had only 40 offensive plays from scrimmage and Rodgers threw for only 181 yards, coach Mike McCarthy's offense was able to run out the final 6½ minutes and deprive Detroit of a final shot at the upset.

It was a costly day for the Packers. Three starters – right tackle Mark Tauscher, middle linebacker Nick Barnett and safety Morgan Burnett – sustained injuries that ended their seasons. ■

OPPOSITE: Cornerback Charles Woodson dives into the end zone over Lions quarterback Shaun Hill after returning an interception 48 yards for a touchdown during the third quarter. Defensive end Mike Neal (96) watches from behind. COREY WILSON/PRESS-GAZETTE

RIGHT: Wide receiver Greg Jennings, right, beats Lions cornerback Jonathan Wade on a 17-yard touchdown pass during the second quarter. COREY WILSON/PRESS-GAZETTE

FAR RIGHT: Linebacker Clay Matthews looks across the line at Lions quarterback Shaun Hill (14). EVAN SIEGLE/PRESS-GAZETTE

BELOW: Quarterback Aaron Rodgers (12) runs the Packers' offense. From left are fullback John Kuhn (30), tight end Tom Crabtree (83), left guard Daryn Colledge (73), center Scott Wells (63), right guard Josh Sitton (71) and right tackle Mark Tauscher (65). It was the last game Tauscher started. He later went on injured reserve with a shoulder injury. EVAN SIEGLE/PRESS-GAZETTE

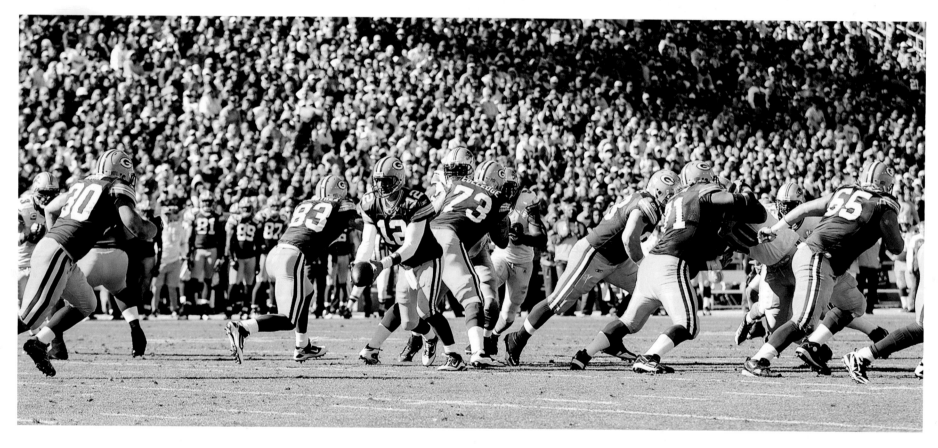

LEFT: Quarterback Aaron Rodgers scrambles past Lions defensive tackle Corey Williams (99), left, and defensive end Cliff Avril (92), right, during the second quarter. COREY WILSON/PRESS-GAZETTE

BOTTOM LEFT: Linebacker Clay Matthews celebrates his sack of Detroit Lions quarterback Shaun Hill during the second quarter. COREY WILSON/PRESS-GAZETTE

BELOW: Cornerback Tramon Williams breaks up a pass intended for Lions wide receiver Bryant Johnson. EVAN SIEGLE/PRESS-GAZETTE

ABOVE: Fans celebrate with wide receiver Greg Jennings after he scored on a 17-yard touchdown pass from Aaron Rodgers during the second quarter. COREY WILSON/PRESS-GAZETTE

OPPOSITE: Fans celebrate after Jennings' touchdown in the second quarter. COREY WILSON/PRESS-GAZETTE

10.4.10 ★
WWW.PACKERSNEWS.COM
GREEN BAY PRESS-GAZETTE

PACKERS**FINAL**

28 ● **26** » Despite a tame win, Packers are 3-1

JUST ENOUGH

Green Bay Packers cornerback Charles Woodson dives into the end zone over Detroit Lions quarterback Shaun Hill after his third-quarter interception on Sunday at Lambeau Field. Woodson returned the interception 48 yards for a touchdown, giving the Packers a 28-14 lead. **Corey Wilson**/Press-Gazette

Dangers lurk in coming weeks after Lions expose Packers' flaws

BY PETE DOUGHERTY
pdougher@greenbaypressgazette.com

AT PACKERSNEWS.COM
Complete coverage of Sunday's game, including photos, stories, commentary and video.

A quarter of the way through the 2010 schedule, the Green Bay Packers are hardly blowing off anybody's doors.

So, what does it mean for their championship aspirations that as a 14½-point favorite they had to hold off the winless Detroit Lions in the final

is right, and the Packers are hitting the part of their schedule where they'll pay a stiffer price if their play doesn't pick up. Over the next six games, the Packers can at Washing

coordinator Dom Capers to back off his zone-blitz repertoire. Hill did that by gashing blitzes with several hot reads and screens to convert long third downs.

That said, Capers' defense helped save the win by keeping Detroit out of the end zone in the second half, leaving the Lions with only four Jason Hanson field goals in their comeback from a

going on. We want to get back to that."

The Packers had their chances to win this game convincingly but didn't have the offensive punch (261 yards in total offense) or care with the ball to put the game away. In the second half, Jordy Nelson had a crucial fumble on a kickoff return, and quarterback Aaron Rodgers had two passes to re-

Washington Redskins

October 10, 2010 • FedEx Field, Landover, Md. • L 16-13 OT

LANDOVER, Md. — All that mattered was Donovan McNabb found a way to win and the Green Bay Packers didn't.

Yards, quality of play, in most ways it's easy to argue the Packers played better football than McNabb's Washington Redskins.

Yet after Mason Crosby bounced a 53-yard field-goal try off the left upright in the final seconds of regulation and Aaron Rodgers threw an interception in overtime, it was Washington and its quarterback who walked off FedEx Field with the victory.

The injuries started to pile up for the Packers with Rodgers sustaining a concussion while getting hit on his overtime interception.

The Packers didn't find a way despite putting up the kind of numbers that often make for lopsided games.

After three quarters, they had a huge edge in yardage (336 to Washington's 181). Their defense, with Charlie Peprah starting at safety and Pat Lee as the No. 3 cornerback, put in a good performance in pressuring McNabb (four sacks, 70.8 passer rating going into the fourth quarter).

There also were Crosby's two missed field goals, a 48-yarder wide right late in the third quarter, then the 53-yarder that hooked into the left upright with 1 second left in regulation.

And there were an astounding seven dropped, drive-killing passes — four by Donald Driver, two by James Jones and one by Jordy Nelson.

Tight end Jermichael Finley, the Packers' playmaking tight end, went down with a knee injury that ended his season. ■

OPPOSITE: Teammates Ryan Pickett (79), Charlie Peprah (26), Nick Collins (36), Charles Woodson (21) and Greg Jennings (85) show support for tight end Jermichael Finley after he injured a knee during the first quarter. Those tending to Finley include team doctor Patrick McKenzie (head visible), trainer Pepper Burruss (pink towel on shoulder) and equipment manager Red Batty (leaning over Burruss). The injury ended Finley's season. COREY WILSON/PRESS-GAZETTE

RIGHT: The Packers defense gets ready as Washington begins a drive on its 1-yard line during the second quarter. Washington gained 32 yards in five plays and punted. COREY WILSON/PRESS-GAZETTE

OPPOSITE TOP LEFT: Linebacker Desmond Bishop, pressures Washington quarterback Donovan McNabb during the fourth quarter. COREY WILSON/PRESS-GAZETTE

OPPOSITE TOP RIGHT: Washington safety LaRon Landry intercepts quarterback Aaron Rodgers in overtime. COREY WILSON/PRESS-GAZETTE

OPPOSITE BOTTOM LEFT: Kicker Mason Crosby (2) reacts after missing a 53-yard field goal that would have won the game with 7 seconds left in the fourth quarter. The kick hit the left upright and bounced away. COREY WILSON/PRESS-GAZETTE

OPPOSITE BOTTOM RIGHT: Cornerback Tramon Williams, center, walks away as Washington kicker Graham Gano (4), holder Hunter Smith (17) and tight end Chris Cooley (47) celebrate Gano's game-winning 33-yard field goal in overtime. COREY WILSON/PRESS-GAZETTE

BOTTOM LEFT: Quarterback Aaron Rodgers (head up at center) is stopped short of the goal line on a sneak play on third down during the second quarter. From left are Washington defensive lineman Phillip Daniels (93), Packers guard Josh Sitton (71), Washington nose tackle Ma'ake Kemoeatu (96) and linebacker Lorenzo Alexander (97) and Packers guard Daryn Colledge (73). The Packers went for it on fourth down, but Rodgers' pass to tight end Andrew Quarless fell incomplete. COREY WILSON/PRESS-GAZETTE

10.11.10 ★
WWW.PACKERSNEWS.COM
GREEN BAY PRESS-GAZETTE

PACKERS**FINAL**

16 🅖13 OT » Woes mount as Packers fall to 3-2

THIS ONE HURTS

Washington Redskins safety LaRon Landry, left, intercepts Green Bay Packers quarterback Aaron Rodgers, right, in overtime Sunday at FedEx Field in Landover, Md. **Corey Wilson/Press-Gazette**

Playmakers go down with Packers as mistakes, injuries pile up

BY PETE DOUGHERTY

Miami Dolphins

October 17, 2010 • Lambeau Field, Green Bay • L 23-20 OT

What happened to the offensive juggernaut that was supposed to be the 2010 Green Bay Packers? It went missing through the first six weeks of the season, at least when it mattered most, such as getting into the end zone when there was a chance to open a decent lead or driving for a game-winning score in overtime.

That was the story at sold-out Lambeau Field, where the Packers' attrition-diminished defense held up well enough to win but where the offense directed by coach Mike McCarthy failed to come through in a loss to the gritty Miami Dolphins.

A glance at the stat sheet hardly told the story. The Packers put up 359 yards in total offense, which usually is a solid day's work.

But aside from an 86-yard touchdown pass to Greg Jennings in the first quarter and a clutch 69-yard touchdown drive in the final 5½ minutes that forced overtime, the Packers' offense was underwhelming for the second straight week and for the third time in three defeats.

Though Aaron Rodgers threw for 313 yards, he had only an 84.5 passer rating, completed barely more than half his passes (18-for-33, 54.5 completion percentage) and was sacked five times.

The Packers weren't able to make Miami pay for its pedestrian quarterback, Chad Henne (23-for-39, 231 yards, 82.3 passer rating), who is too scattershot to be a playmaker.

On the stat sheet, it was as rough a day for the Packers' defense, which gave up 381 yards and allowed Miami offensive coordinator Dan Henning to grind the clock with a conservative game plan featuring two physical backs in Ronnie Brown (19 carries for 73 yards) and Ricky Williams (13 for 64).

Dolphins receiver Brandon Marshall, who used his Terrell Owens-type size and speed to make 10 catches for 127 yards. ■

OPPOSITE: Quarterback Aaron Rodgers reacts after throwing an interception during the third quarter. EVAN SIEGLE/PRESS-GAZETTE

ABOVE: Wide receiver Greg Jennings, left, makes an 86-yard touchdown catch against Dolphins cornerback Vontae Davis during the first quarter. COREY WILSON/PRESS-GAZETTE

RIGHT: Linebackers Desmond Bishop (55) and Brady Poppinga (51) stuff Dolphins wide receiver Davone Bess (15) during the second quarter. Safety Charlie Peprah (26) assists. EVAN SIEGLE/PRESS-GAZETTE

BELOW: Dolphins receiver Brian Hartline dives over linebacker Brad Jones after a catch during the second quarter. COREY WILSON/PRESS-GAZETTE

ABOVE: Quarterback Aaron Rodgers gives orders to his teammates at the line of scrimmage during the fourth quarter. EVAN SIEGLE/PRESS-GAZETTE

LEFT: Packers cheerleaders work the crowd in the south end zone during the fourth quarter. COREY WILSON/PRESS-GAZETTE

FAR LEFT: Wide receiver Greg Jennings tries to elude a Dolphins defender after making a catch during the fourth quarter. EVAN SIEGLE/PRESS-GAZETTE

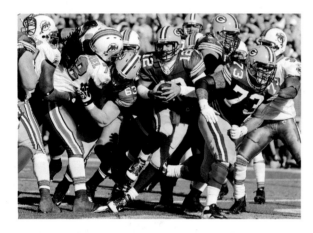

ABOVE: Quarterback Aaron Rodgers (12) sneaks into the end zone behind left guard Daryn Colledge (73) to score on a 1-yard run and tie the game with 13 seconds left in the fourth quarter. Center Scott Wells (63) blocks Dolphins nose tackle Tony McDaniel (78) at left. COREY WILSON/PRESS-GAZETTE

TOP: Quarterback Aaron Rodgers, center, is stopped at the Miami 1-yard line by Dolphins safety Chris Clemons (left center) and cornerback Jason Allen (obscured) after an 8-yard run late in the fourth quarter. Packers wide receiver Donald Driver at left. Dolphins cornerback Sean Smith (24) is in the foreground COREY WILSON/PRESS-GAZETTE

RIGHT: Wide receiver Greg Jennings, left, celebrates with quarterback Aaron Rodgers after Rodgers' game-tying, 1-yard sneak for a touchdown late in the fourth quarter. COREY WILSON/PRESS-GAZETTE

LEFT: With linebacker Brad Jones (58) reaching highest, the Packers' defensive unit tries to block Dolphins kicker Dan Carpenter's game-winning field goal in overtime. EVAN SIEGLE/PRESS-GAZETTE

BELOW LEFT: Dolphins kicker Dan Carpenter (5) is hugged by long snapper John Denney (92) after Carpenter kicked the game-winning field goal in overtime. Dolphins tackle Vernon Carey (72) celebrates at right. EVAN SIEGLE/PRESS-GAZETTE

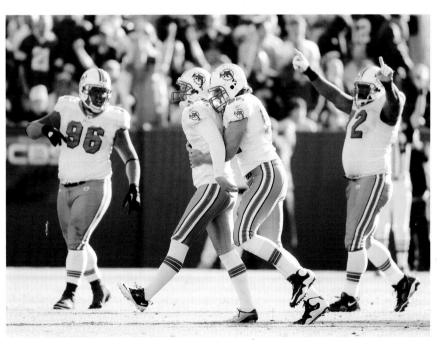

10.18.10
WWW.PACKERSNEWS.COM
GREEN BAY PRESS-GAZETTE

PACKERS FINAL

23 · 20 OT » Back to middle of pack at 3-3

REPEAT DEFEAT

Miami Dolphins receiver Brian Hartline dives over Green Bay Packers linebacker Brad Jones after a second-quarter catch on Sunday at Lambeau Field. **Corey Wilson/Press-Gazette**

Frustration builds as offense again sputters in clutch

BY PETE DOUGHERTY
pdougherty@greenbaypressgazette.com

Where is the offensive juggernaut that was supposed to be the 2010 Green Bay Packers?

Nowhere through the first six weeks of the season, at least not when it matters most, such as getting into the end zone when there's a chance to open a decent lead or driving for the game-winning score in overtime.

That was the story Sunday at mid-out Lambeau Field, where the Packers' attrition-diminished defense held up well enough to win but where the coach Mike McCarthy-led offense failed to come through in a 23-20 loss to the gritty Miami Dolphins.

"It's hard to lose, period," McCarthy said. "It's hard to lose home games. To lose overtime games — particularly

Though Rodgers threw for 313 yards, he had only an 84.5 passer rating, completed barely more than half his passes (18-for-33, 54.5 completion percentage) and was sacked five times. His bomb to Jennings was pinpoint, and he made two big plays in that game-tying drive — a scramble and across-the-body throw to Jordy Nelson for a 14-yard gain that converted a third down, and a dart to Jennings for 20 yards that converted a fourth down. But those kinds of plays, which seemed almost routine the second half of last year, have been relatively infrequent in 2010.

Instead, there have been missed chances. Such as late in the third quarter, when Jennings got behind the safeties on a post pattern but Rodgers instead threw over Nelson's head on a shorter out pattern to the left. Or early in the fourth quarter, when Nelson

Minnesota Vikings

October 24, 2010 • Lambeau Field, Green Bay • W 28-24

They needed an overturned replay challenge and a tough stop in the final seconds from their defense, but the Green Bay Packers did it. They beat Brett Favre.

After getting swept by Favre and the Minnesota Vikings last season, the Packers stood strong in front of a national TV audience. They turned back Favre's fourth-quarter rally in a gritty win over their bitter rival.

Last year, the Vikings swept the Packers behind Favre's sharp play plus a vicious pass rush that sacked quarterback Aaron Rodgers 14 times in the two games combined. This time, the Packers were able to turn around both of those problems.

Though Favre at times was able to stand comfortably in the pocket, his 50.4 passer rating reflected the occasional effectiveness of the Packers' rush. After not intercepting Favre last year, they got him three times in the second half.

In the waning moments, Favre appeared poised to break the hearts of the Packers and their fans when he connected with wide receiver Percy Harvin for an apparent miracle throw and catch that would have given Minnesota the lead. The officials on the field ruled the play a touchdown, but Harvin clearly came down with one foot out of bounds. Packers coach Mike McCarthy's replay challenge led to the call being overturned.

Although Rodgers didn't have a huge game, it was good enough (295 yards passing, two touchdowns, two interceptions) to lift the weight of the two losses to the Vikings last season. ∎

OPPOSITE: Linebacker Desmond Bishop returns an interception 32 yards for a touchdown during the third quarter. Vikings wide receiver Randy Moss gives chase. EVAN SIEGLE/PRESS-GAZETTE

ABOVE: A young Packers fans cheers during the first quarter. EVAN SIEGLE/PRESS-GAZETTE

ABOVE RIGHT: A Packers fan and a Vikings fan walk together before the game. EVAN SIEGLE/PRESS-GAZETTE

RIGHT: Running back Brandon Jackson scores on a 1-yard touchdown run during the first quarter. EVAN SIEGLE/PRESS-GAZETTE

ABOVE: Coach Mike McCarthy challenges an apparent touchdown catch by Vikings tight end Visanthe Shiancoe during the second quarter. The touchdown was overturned. EVAN SIEGLE/PRESS-GAZETTE

ABOVE RIGHT: Vikings quarterback Brett Favre reacts after an apparent touchdown pass to tight end Visanthe Shiancoe was challenged and overturned during the second quarter. EVAN SIEGLE/PRESS-GAZETTE

RIGHT: Tight end Andrew Quarless catches a 9-yard touchdown pass against Vikings safety Tyrell Johnson and another defender during the second quarter. COREY WILSON/PRESS-GAZETTE

RIGHT: Quarterback Aaron Rodgers throws a pass during the third quarter. Center Scott Wells (63) is at left. COREY WILSON/PRESS-GAZETTE

BOTTOM LEFT: Vikings guard Anthony Herrera (64) tries to tackle linebacker A.J. Hawk as he returns an interception during the third quarter. EVAN SIEGLE/PRESS-GAZETTE

BELOW RIGHT: Wide receiver Greg Jennings catches a pass for a 14-yard touchdown in front of Vikings cornerback Asher allen during the third quarter. EVAN SIEGLE/PRESS-GAZETTE

10.25.10
WWW.PACKERSNEWS.COM
GREEN BAY **PRESS-GAZETTE**

PACKERS**FINAL**

28 ● **24** » Packers tied for NFC North lead at 4-3

FINALLY, FAVRE FOILED

Green Bay Packers linebacker Desmond Bishop, left, scores a touchdown after returning a Brett Favre interception 32 yards during the third quarter Sunday night at Lambeau Field. The interception was Favre's second of three in the game and gave the Packers a 28-17 lead. **Corey Wilson/Press-Gazette**

Packers survive last-minute drive to top rival Vikings on 'special night'

BY PETE DOUGHERTY
pdougherty@greenbaypressgazette.com

They needed an overturned touchdown and a tough stop in the final seconds from their defense, but the Green Bay Packers did it. They beat Brett Favre.

After getting swept by Favre and the Minnesota Vikings last season, the Packers stood strong in front of a national TV audience to turn back Favre's fourth-quarter rally and else their NFC

"It was an excellent team win and an excellent character win," coach Mike McCarthy said. "Something this team needed."

The win, which came after the Packers had lost back-to-back games, puts them at 4-3 as they close in on the halfway point of the season, and tied for first place in the division with Chicago, which lost to Washington. Minnesota dropped to 3-4 and is on the brink of getting chased out of the division race with a tough game coming up

the season," quarterback Aaron Rodgers said in describing his feelings. "We were 3-3 coming in, a division opponent, our greatest rival, close score, the way it ended. It was a special night for us."

Last year, the Vikings swept the Packers behind Favre's ultra-sharp play plus a vicious pass rush that sacked Rodgers 14 times in the two games combined. But the Packers were able to turn around both of those problems in this game.

rush. Even with a defensive line that lost Cullen Jenkins (calf strain) in warm-ups and Ryan Pickett (ankle) in the first quarter, the Packers got to Favre for one sack, several key pressures and drew a critical penalty when tackle Phil Loadholt grabbed Clay Matthews' face mask after the outside linebacker blew around him, which set the Vikings back 15 yards when they appeared on the brink of the go-ahead touchdown late in the game.

ABOVE: Linebacker Clay Matthews pauses for a moment after stopping Vikings running back Adrian Peterson on Minnesota's last drive during the fourth quarter. COREY WILSON/PRESS-GAZETTE

TOP: Linebacker Desmond Bishop tackles Vikings quarterback Brett Favre during the fourth quarter. COREY WILSON/PRESS-GAZETTE

LEFT: Linebacker Clay Matthews grabs the jersey of Vikings quarterback Brett Favre during the fourth quarter. COREY WILSON/PRESS-GAZETTE

New York Jets

October 31, 2010 • New Meadowlands Stadium, East Rutherford, N.J. • W 9-0

EAST RUTHERFORD, N.J. — How about that? The Green Bay Packers won a game with defense and special teams.

Shrugging off injuries in their defensive front seven, the Packers went on the road and stopped one of the NFL's premier run games, prevailed in the battle of field position on the leg of their heretofore shaky punter and took out the swaggering New York Jets for their third shutout of the Mike McCarthy era. It was their first road shutout since 1991.

It was about as big as mid-season wins get, putting the Packers back in first place in the NFC North.

The Jets were the self-proclaimed best team in the NFL and came in on a five-game winning streak and rested from their bye.

The battered Packers, on the other hand, had just placed starting outside linebacker Brad Jones and backup defensive end Mike Neal on injured reserve and were playing without starting defensive end Ryan Pickett, who was out with an ankle injury for the fourth straight game.

But Green Bay showed how NFL teams can overcome injuries and keep a season alive.

The Packers didn't do much of anything on offense and were substantially outgained (360 to 237 yards), but that doesn't mean they were outplayed. They held the upper hand from late in the first quarter until the end. They did it with a stout run defense and three huge takeaways — an interception and fumble recovery by cornerback Tramon Williams and an interception by cornerback Charles Woodson.

First-year punter Tim Masthay complemented the defense with his best day since winning the job in training camp. His excellent 41.5-yard net average only told part of the story of the quality of his work on eight punts. When the game was a scoreless battle of field position in the first quarter, his net punts of 55, 48 and 51 yards tilted the field in the Packers' favor.. ■

OPPOSITE: Linebacker Brandon Chillar sacks Jets quarterback Mark Sanchez during the first quarter. COREY WILSON/PRESS-GAZETTE

ABOVE: Safety Charlie Peprah (26 at right) loses his helmet as he and linebacker Frank Zombo (58) and Desmond Bishop (55) stop Jets running back LaDainian Tomlinson during the first quarter. COREY WILSON/PRESS-GAZETTE

RIGHT: Cover man Pat Lee tackles the Jets' Jim Leonhard on a punt return during the first quarter. COREY WILSON/PRESS-GAZETTE

BELOW: Cornerback Tramon Williams (38) intercepts a pass intended for Jets receiver Jerricho Cotchery during the second quarter. Linebacker Brandon Chillar is at left. COREY WILSON/PRESS-GAZETTE

ABOVE: Cornerback Tramon Williams jogs along the sideline, trailed by safety Nick Collins, after making an interception against Jets quarterback Mark Sanchez during the second quarter. COREY WILSON/PRESS-GAZETTE

ABOVE: Nose tackle B.J. Raji (90) and linebacker A.J. Hawk (50) roll over Jets running back LaDainian Tomlinson during the fourth quarter. COREY WILSON/PRESS-GAZETTE

ABOVE RIGHT: Quarterback Aaron Rodgers ducks away from Jets defensive end Jason Taylor during the second quarter. COREY WILSON/PRESS-GAZETTE

BELOW RIGHT: Cornerback Charles Woodson jogs off the field after making an interception against Jets quarterback Mark Sanchez during the fourth quarter. COREY WILSON/PRESS-GAZETTE

PACKERS**FINAL**

9 **0** » Packers swagger home at 5-3

SHUTOUT IS SWEET TREAT

Green Bay Packers linebacker Desmond Bishop, left, stuffs New York Jets running back LaDainian Tomlinson during the third quarter of Sunday's game at New Meadowlands Stadium in East Rutherford, N.J. **Photos by Corey Wilson/Press-Gazette**

Defense, special teams humble high-flying Jets in key road win

BY PETE DOUGHERTY
pdougher@greenbaypressgazette.com

EAST RUTHERFORD, N.J. — How about that? The Green Bay Packers won a game with defense and special teams.

Injuries in the defensive front seven be damned, the Packers went on the road and stopped one of the NFL's premier run games, prevailed in the battle of field position on the leg of their heretofore shaky punter and took out the swaggering New York Jets 9-0 at New Meadowlands Stadium on Sunday afternoon.

"Every week you come out with a win is huge, and to do it today with a shutout is even bigger," Packers safety Nick Collins said. "Who would ever thought that little ol' Green Bay could come in here and beat the New York Jets with all the hype they have, all the big names?"

In its own way, this is about as big as midseason wins get. The Jets were the self-proclaimed best team in the NFL and came in on a five-game winning streak and rested from their bye. The battered Packers, on the other hand, had just this week placed two defensive regulars (starting linebacker Brad Jones and backup end Mike Neal) on injured reserve and were playing without starting defensive end Ryan Pickett (ankle) for the fourth straight game.

But the Packers showed how NFL teams can overcome injuries and keep a season alive, in this case with a close-to-the-vest win that improves them to 5-3 and leaves them a half-game ahead of the 4-3 Chicago Bears, who were on their bye, in the NFC North Division.

Packers cornerback Charles Woodson, left, laughs with teammate Nick Collins after his interception of Jets quarterback Mark Sanchez during the fourth quarter.

The Packers didn't do much of anything on offense and were substantially outgained (380 to 237 yards), but that doesn't mean they were outplayed. They held the upper hand from late in the first quarter until the end, and they did it with a stout run defense and three huge takeaways — an interception and fumble recovery by cornerback Tramon Williams and an interception by cornerback Charles Woodson.

They forced the Jets to put the game in the hands of second-year quarterback Mark Sanchez, who proved he's not ready to carry an offense when it flounders, though he also was victim of several key drops by Jets receivers in the second half. Regardless, the Packers attained their third shutout of the Mike McCarthy era and first road shutout since 1991.

"It's a big win for us, a real big win," quarterback Aaron Rodgers said. "One of the biggest I've been a part of in my time here to go on the road and beat a great team like this. Obviously, offensively we would have liked to do a little bit better, but our defense played incredible."

The Packers' makeshift defensive front handled one of the league's premier offensive lines and held halfbacks LaDainian Tomlinson and Shonn Greene to a combined 76 yards on 22 carries. Tomlinson's 3.4-yard average was almost a full two yards less than his season average of 5.3 yards, and Greene's 3.7-yard average was down from his 4.5 yards.

Nose tackle B.J. Raji, the lone healthy starter on the defensive line, played almost every snap. Rookie C.J. Wilson played regularly for the second straight week, starting end Cullen Jenkins chipped in about 30 snaps playing on a sore calf, and even bulky newcomer Howard Green (6-2, 340 pounds) saw regular action in defensive coordinator Dom Capers' 3-4 base defense.

➤ See Packers, Page 8

AT PACKERSNEWS.COM

Complete coverage of Sunday's game, including photos, stories, commentary and video.

ABOVE: Coach Mike McCarthy, left, greets Jets coach Rex Ryan after the game. COREY WILSON/PRESS-GAZETTE

Dallas Cowboys

November 7, 2010 • Lambeau Field, Green Bay • W 45-7

For the first time all season, the Green Bay Packers looked like one of the elite offenses in the NFL. Facing a crumbling team that seemingly had given up on its coach and its season, the Packers dominated in every way in humiliating the Dallas Cowboys for their third straight win in front of 70,913 spectators at Lambeau Field plus a national Sunday night TV audience.

The Packers dominated in every way imaginable against a Dallas team that fired coach Wade Phillips the next day.

Not only were the Cowboys playing their second game without starting quarterback Tony Romo, who was out with a broken collarbone, but their formerly formidable defense had fallen to No. 27 in the NFL in points allowed, and in its last two games had given up 76 points combined to the New York Giants and Jacksonville Jaguars.

The Packers' No. 16-ranked offense had been looking to find a rhythm playing without halfback Ryan Grant since the opener and tight end Jermichael Finley for most of the season, pounced. Quarterback Aaron Rodgers was sharp and receiver James Jones had a career game, leading a balanced offense with extended playing time in place of the injured Donald Driver.

Combined with one touchdown by safety Nick Collins on a 26-yard fumbled kickoff return and another on outside linebacker Clay Matthews' 62-yard interception return to close out the scoring early in the fourth quarter, the Packers had an easy and satisfying win.

Rodgers finished with a passer rating of 131.5 points (27-for-34 passing for 289 yards and two touchdowns) and also had five scrambles for 41 yards, including a big 27-yarder on a third down that set up the Packers' first touchdown. ■

OPPOSITE: Wide receiver Greg Jennings makes a 33-yard catch against Cowboys cornerback Mike Jenkins during the second quarter. EVAN SIEGLE/PRESS-GAZETTE

ABOVE: Cowboys coach Wade Phillips, right, reacts during the game. He was fired the next day. EVAN SIEGLE/PRESS-GAZETTE

ABOVE RIGHT: Nose tackle Howard Green (95) works against Cowboys guard Kyle Kosier. Green was picked up on waivers at midseason and proved to be a valuable addition to the defense. COREY WILSON/PRESS-GAZETTE

RIGHT: Linebacker Clay Matthews sacks Cowboys quarterback Jon Kitna. EVAN SIEGLE/PRESS-GAZETTE

11.8.10 ★
WWW.PACKERSNEWS.COM
GREEN BAY PRESS-GAZETTE

PACKERS**FINAL**

G 45 ★ 7 » Packers roll into bye week at 6-3

TEXAS-SIZED WHOOPING

ABOVE: Green Bay Packers receiver Greg Jennings makes a catch against Dallas Cowboys cornerback Mike Jenkins during Sunday night's game at Lambeau Field. **Photos by Evan Siegle/Press-Gazette**
LEFT: Packers quarterback Aaron Rodgers reacts after throwing an 8-yard touchdown pass to Jennings in the second quarter.

Offense comes out shooting in 'complete' game

BY PETE DOUGHERTY
pdougher@greenbaypressgazette.com

For the first time in the 2010 season, the Green Bay Packers looked like one of the elite offenses in the NFL.

Facing a crumbling team that has given up on its coach and its season, the Packers dominated in every way Sunday night in humiliating the Dallas Cowboys 45-7 in front of 70,913 spectators at Lambeau Field plus a national TV audience.

"You always set out to play a complete game, and we accomplished that tonight," coach Mike McCarthy said.

pass ratio was tonight. Third down was the key. We played a complete football game tonight. This is the way you want to go into the bye week."

The win is the Packers' third straight and improved their record to 6-3, which keeps them a half-game ahead of Chicago (5-3) and 2½ games ahead of Minnesota (3-5) for first place in the NFC North Division. The Packers also go into their bye week tied with New Orleans at only one-half game behind Atlanta (6-2) and the New York Giants (6-2) for the best record in the NFC.

"You never want to lose going into a bye week," outside linebacker Clay

a little bit and then once we get back it's all business."

The Packers dominated in every way imaginable against a 1-7 Dallas team that was easy pickings as it imploded before the world's eyes. Not only were the Cowboys playing their second game without starting quarterback Tony Romo, who's out with a broken collarbone, but their formerly formidable defense had fallen to No. 27 in the NFL in points allowed, and worse yet in its last two games had given up 76 points combined to the Giants and Jaguars.

» See Packers, Page 3

ABOVE: Linebacker Clay Matthews (52) turns toward the end zone after intercepting a deflected pass from Cowboys quarterback jon Kitna (3) during the fourth quarter. He's accompanied by linebacker A.J. Hawk (50) and chased by Cowboys tackle Marc Columbo (75). Matthews returned it 62 yards for a touchdown.

EVAN SIEGLE/PRESS-GAZETTE

FAR LEFT: Cornerback Tramon Williams tips a ball away from Cowboys wide receiver Dez Bryant during the third quarter.

COREY WILSON/PRESS-GAZETTE

Minnesota Vikings

November 21, 2010 • Hubert H. Humphrey Metrodome, Minneapolis • W 31-3

MINNEAPOLIS — Silence is the sweet sound of victory for any visitor at the Metrodome. Never had it come earlier or with more satisfaction for the Green Bay Packers, when with 55 seconds left in the third quarter, they got the ball back with a 21-point lead over the archrival Minnesota Vikings.

As quarterback Aaron Rodgers and his offense approached the line of scrimmage, there was nothing. No Viking horn. No chest-rattling music. No nothing.

The Rollerdome, as former Bears coach Mike Ditka contemptuously called it, maybe the loudest venue in the NFL, might as well have been empty, numbed as it was by the Packers' domination.

The victory, the largest margin for the Packers in the Metrodome since it opened in 1982, accomplished so much in one shot.

It capped a satisfying sweep of quarterback Brett Favre and the Vikings, a year after Favre humbled the Packers with a sweep of two hot-blooded games that were the difference in the NFC North race.

It sent the crumbling Vikings into further disarray, dropping them to 3-7 and essentially ending their faint playoff hopes.

It also triggered a stadium-wide "Fi-re Chil-dress" chant aimed at Minnesota coach Brad Childress with about 9 minutes left in the game.

Childress was fired the next day. ∎

OPPOSITE: Vikings quarterback Brett Favre shows his frustration after failing to complete a pass on third down during the first quarter. COREY WILSON/PRESS-GAZETTE

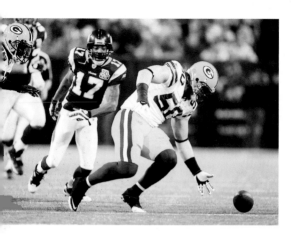

ABOVE: Linebacker A.J. Hawk (50) chases a loose ball after cornerback Charles Woodson stripped it from Vikings running back Toby Gerhart during the second quarter. Safety Nick Collins (36) and Vikings wide receiver Greg Lewis (17) trail the play. EVAN SIEGLE/PRESS-GAZETTE

RIGHT: Defensive end Cullen Jenkins (77) and nose tackle B.J. Raji (90) hit Vikings quarterback Brett Favre during the first quarter. EVAN SIEGLE/PRESS-GAZETTE

LEFT: Wide receiver James Jones makes a 3-yard touchdown catch against Vikings cornerback Chris Cook during the second quarter. EVAN SIEGLE/PRESS-GAZETTE

FAR LEFT: Wide receiver Greg Jennings makes a leaping catch over Vikings cornerback Chris Cook during the second quarter. EVAN SIEGLE/PRESS-GAZETTE

BELOW LEFT: Coach Mike McCarthy talks with long snapper Brett Goode during the second quarter. EVAN SIEGLE/PRESS-GAZETTE

BELOW : Cornerback Tramon Williams levels Vikings receiver Greg Lewis and forces an incompletion during the second quarter. COREY WILSON/PRESS-GAZETTE

PACKERSFINAL

G 31 V 3 » Packers keep pace in NFC North at 7-3

SWEEP SATISFACTION

Green Bay Packers defensive end Cullen Jenkins (77) and nose tackle B.J. Raji, left, put a hit on Minnesota Vikings quarterback Brett Favre in the first quarter of Sunday's game at the Metrodome in Minneapolis. The Packers' defense held Favre to a 51.2 quarterback rating in the game. **Evan Siegle/Press-Gazette**

Dominant Packers silence crumbling Vikings at Metrodome

BY PETE DOUGHERTY
pdougher@greenbaypressgazette.com

MINNEAPOLIS — Silence is the

by the Packers' domination in their 31-3 win.

"It was pretty cool," defensive end Cullen Jenkins said of the moment. "Seemed like the whole demeanor and

pace with the Chicago Bears for first place in the NFC North Division.

It also capped a satisfying sweep of quarterback Brett Favre and the Vikings, a year after Favre humbled

This is hardly what the 41-year-old Favre imagined when he decided in August to return to the Vikings.

"Nope," he said. "I know you want me to elaborate on it. This has got me

ABOVE: Ragnar, the Vikings' mascot, congratulates Packers quarterback Aaron Rodgers after the game. Ragnar's real name is Joe Juranich. He was born in Milwaukee. EVAN SIEGLE/PRESS-GAZETTE

OPPOSITE: Wide receiver Greg Jennings spins around Vikings cornerback Asher Allen on his way to score a 46-yard touchdown during the third quarter. COREY WILSON/PRESS-GAZETTE

Atlanta Falcons

November 28, 2010 • Georgia Dome, Atlanta • L 20-17

ATLANTA – Not much separated NFC contenders the Atlanta Falcons and Green Bay Packers at the Georgia Dome in their first meeting, though plenty separated them in the NFC playoff race after the Falcons won.

Falcons coach Mike Smith's disciplined team steadfastly refused to make the big mistake for the 60 full minutes. That only magnified the Packers' lone big error, a goal-line fumble by quarterback Aaron Rodgers, in the second quarter.

In a wire-to-wire game that featured Rodgers and the Falcons' Matt Ryan in a duel of top young quarterbacks, that helped give Atlanta a winning edge, which it seized when kicker Matt Bryant knocked through a 47-yard field goal with 9 seconds left for a three-point win.

It was hardly backbreaking for the Packers to lose on a last-second field goal to an Atlanta team that is 21-3 at the Georgia Dome with Smith as coach, including 19-1 with Ryan at quarterback.

Against most teams, Rodgers' performance (114.5 passer rating, 344 yards passing, no interceptions) would have been good enough to win, but Ryan was his passing equal (108.0 rating) and played mistake-free.

The Packers never even came close to intercepting Ryan. His 85.7 percent completion rate (24-for-28) was in part a function of throwing mostly short passes, but he also never forced things when the Packers' coverages took the NFL's leading receiver, Roddy White, out of the game.

The most glaring difference between these teams was the run game. The Packers had enough bad runs early that coach Mike McCarthy mostly abandoned the run by the second half. Halfback Brandon Jackson gained 26 yards on 10 carries.

The Falcons, on the other hand, regularly pounded Michael Turner at the Packers' front seven, and the 247-pounder shed tackler after tackler on his way to 110 yards rushing and a 4.8-yard average. ∎

OPPOSITE: Wide receiver Greg Jennings kneels after failing to score on the last play of the game. From left are Falcons safety William Moore and Packers nose tackle B.J. Raji (90), wide receiver James Jones (89) and guard Daryn Colledge (73). Jennings caught a 35-yard pass from quarterback Aaron Rodgers, but fumbled out of bounds while trying to lateral the ball. COREY WILSON/PRESS-GAZETTE

ABOVE: Linebacker Frank Zombo sacks Falcons quarterback Matt Ryan during the first quarter. COREY WILSON/PRESS-GAZETTE

ABOVE LEFT: Linebacker Desmond Bishop, left, tackles Falcons running back Michael Turner during the first quarter. Defensive end Ryan Pickett is on the bottom of the pile. COREY WILSON/PRESS-GAZETTE

LEFT: Linebacker Brandon Chillar (54) injured a shoulder while tackling Falcons kick returner Eric Weems (14) during the first quarter. The injury ended Chillar's season COREY WILSON/PRESS-GAZETTE

ABOVE: Falcons linebacker Mike Peterson, center, grabs a fumble by quarterback Aaron Rodgers near the end zone during the second quarter. From bottom left, Packers center Scott Wells (63) and guards Josh Sitton and Daryn Colledge (73) also go for the ball, as does defensive end Chauncey Davis (92). COREY WILSON/PRESS-GAZETTE

LEFT: Coach Mike McCarthy watches the action during the third quarter. Linebacker Clay Matthews is at left. COREY WILSON/PRESS-GAZETTE

RIGHT: Safety Charlie Peprah stops Falcons tight end Tony Gonzalez short of the goal line during the fourth quarter. COREY WILSON/PRESS-GAZETTE

OPPOSITE LEFT: Falcons tight end Tony Gonzalez jumps into the arms of running back Michael Turner after Turner ran for a 1-yard touchdown during the fourth quarter. COREY WILSON/PRESS-GAZETTE

OPPOSITE TOP RIGHT: Wide receiver Jordy Nelson spikes the ball after scoring on a 10-yard touchdown pass to tie the game at 17 with 56 seconds left in the fourth quarter. Falcons safety Thomas DeCoud is at left. COREY WILSON/PRESS-GAZETTE

OPPOSITE BOTTOM RIGHT: Falcons kicker Matt Bryant (3) makes a 47-yard field goal to win the game with 9 seconds left in the fourth quarter. COREY WILSON/PRESS-GAZETTE

63

San Francisco 49ers

December 5, 2010 • Lambeau Field, Green Bay • W 34-16

The Green Bay Packers came out on a blustery, cold day at Lambeau Field and did what they had to, beating an inferior team in a bad-weather game.

The San Francisco 49ers weren't bereft of talent with Vernon Davis at tight end and Michael Crabtree at receiver, but they couldn't match up with the Packers at quarterback or on defense.

The 49ers were exposed for what they were: A below-average team that was on the fringe of the playoff chase only because it plays in the NFL's worst division, the NFC West.

The Packers won comfortably behind another efficient performance by Aaron Rodgers, a couple of big plays by receivers Greg Jennings and Donald Driver, and a stout defense that kept San Francisco from running the ball, the one thing that would have given it a chance.

As the game went on, Rodgers' passing improved as he adapted to the conditions for a 70.0 completion percentage (21-for-30). The offense also got some help from a new source, sixth-round draft pick James Starks. In his NFL debut, the rookie shot past Brandon Jackson as the team's primary running back.

The 49ers, on the other hand, never got a running game going without injured halfback Frank Gore. His replacements, Brian Westbrook and Anthony Dixon, combined for 64 yards on 18 carries.

Quarterback Troy Smith, who won three of his four previous starts, was unable to carry the offense without that help on the ground. His 64.4 passer rating included a scattershot 40 percent (10-for-25) completion rate. ∎

OPPOSITE: Sam Shields leaps through an opening between cover men Phillip Adams (35) and NaVorro Bowman (53) while returning a kick during the first quarter. EVAN SIEGLE/PRESS-GAZETTE

PACKERS**FINAL**

G **34** 49 **16** »» Packers keep pace in playoff race

GETTING THE JOB DONE

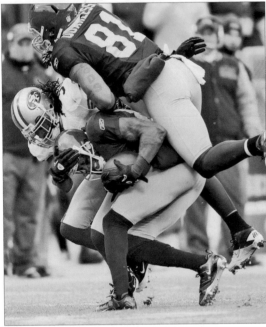

Green Bay Packers receiver Donald Driver (80) keeps his balance as he collides with Packers tight end Andrew Quarless (81) and San Francisco 49ers safety Dashon Goldson (38) after making a catch in the third quarter Sunday at Lambeau Field. Driver scored on the play. **Evan Siegle/Press-Gazette**

Packers bowl over 49ers behind big plays, defense

BY PETE DOUGHERTY
pdougher@greenbaypressgazette.com

The Green Bay Packers came out on a blustery, cold day at Lambeau Field and did what they had to: beat an inferior team going toe to toe in a bad-weather game.

The San Francisco 49ers aren't bereft of talent with Vernon Davis at tight end and Michael Crabtree at receiver, but they couldn't match up with the Packers at quarterback or on defense and were exposed for what they are: a below-average team that's on the fringe of the playoff chase only because it plays in the NFL's worst division, the NFC West.

The Packers ended up winning comfortably 34-16, behind another efficient performance by Aaron Rodgers, a couple of big plays by receivers Greg Jennings and Donald Driver and a stout defense that kept San Francisco from doing the one thing that would have

AT PACKERSNEWS.COM

Get our complete online wrapup of Sunday's game, including:
■ Our photos from the game
■ **Video:** Kareem Copeland's analysis of Sunday's victory
■ Kareem's postgame chat with readers

given it a chance, that is, running the ball.

"We out-physicaled a team that prides itself on being physical," defensive end Ryan Pickett said. "Felt like we came out and played more physical than them, especially up front. Their line, watching them on tape, they got a lot of push, they pushed around a lot of the teams. That came right down our alley. They tried to play power ball with us, and we stopped 'em."

This was a must win for the Packers, just as it will be next week when they face the 2-10 Detroit Lions. At 8-4, the Packers will face a tough three-game stretch to close the season at New England and at home against the New York Giants and Chicago, so they can't afford to slip up against the two lesser teams left on their schedule in their chase for the playoffs.

The win keeps the Packers one game behind the NFC North Division-leading Bears, whose come-from-behind victory at Detroit pushed their record to 9-3. With one playoff spot reserved for an NFC West champion that probably will be .500 at best, the Packers are one of seven clubs fighting for five playoff spots: Atlanta is on top at 10-2, followed by New Orleans and Chicago at 9-3; Philadelphia, the Giants and Packers at 8-4; and Tampa Bay at 7-5.

"Eight-and-four, pretty good record so far," cornerback Tramon Williams said. "But we've got a long ways to go. We all in here know that. Everyone's up for the challenge."

The Packers didn't jump on the 49ers

right away on a day when the winds blew from the northwest at 16 mph and made the 36-degree day feel like 14 degree. But as the game went on, Rodgers' passing only improved as he adapted to the conditions for a 70.0 completion percentage (21-for-30), and the offense got some help from a new source, sixth-round draft pick James Starks, who in his NFL debut shot past Brandon Jackson as the team's primary back.

The 49ers, on the other hand, never got a running game going without injured halfback Frank Gore — his replacements, Brian Westbrook and Anthony Dixon, combined for 64 yards on 18 carries. And quarterback Troy Smith, winner of three of his four previous starts with the 49ers, was unable to carry the offense without that help on the ground. His 64.4 passer rating included a scattershot 40 percent (10-for-25) completion rate.

► See Packers, Page 5

RIGHT: Wide receiver Donald Driver, center, goes head to head with 49ers safety Dashon Goldson to score on a 61-yard touchdown during the third quarter. Driver broke several tackles on his way to the end zone. COREY WILSON/PRESS-GAZETTE

BELOW: Quarterback Aaron Rodgers and the rest of the Packers wore the team's new third uniform in the game. The blue jersey with gold numbers, khaki-colored pants and brown helmets were modeled after the Packers' uniforms of the late 1920s and early 1930s. EVAN SIEGLE/PRESS-GAZETTE

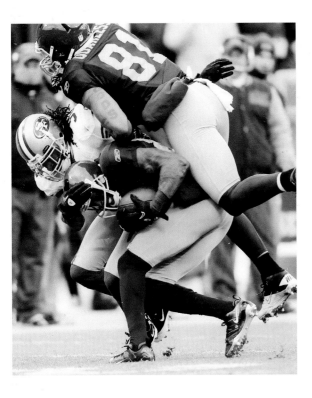

ABOVE: Wide receiver Donald Driver (80) keeps his balance as he collides with tight end Andrew Quarless (81) and 49ers safety Dashon Goldson (38) after making a catch during the third quarter. Driver scored a 61-yard touchdown on the play, breaking several tackles. EVAN SIEGLE/PRESS-GAZETTE

ABOVE RIGHT: Linebacker Clay Matthews, right, brings down 49ers fullback Delanie Walker with help from safety Charlie Peprah during the fourth quarter. COREY WILSON/PRESS-GAZETTE

RIGHT: Quarterback Aaron Rodgers slides for a first down in front of 49ers safety Sashon Goldson during the fourth quarter. COREY WILSON/PRESS-GAZETTE

FAR RIGHT: Nose tackle B.J. Raji sacks 49ers quarterback Troy Smith during the fourth quarter. EVAN SIEGLE/PRESS-GAZETTE

ABOVE: Backup quarterback Matt Flynn (10) is all smiles as he takes the field during the fourth quarter. EVAN SIEGLE/PRESS-GAZETTE

RIGHT: Defensive end Cullen Jenkins limps off the field with a calif injury during the fourth quarter. The injury kept Jenkins out for the last four games of the regular season. COREY WILSON/PRESS-GAZETTE

OPPOSITE: Running back James Starks (44) looks for room to run after escaping from linebacker Patrick Willis (52) during the fourth quarter. Defensive tackle Demetric Evans (93) gives chase. EVAN SIEGLE/PRESS-GAZETTE

Detroit Lions

December 12, 2010 • Ford Field, Detroit • L 7-3

DETROIT — Aaron Rodgers took another blow to the head and the Green Bay Packers took a blow to their ego, if not their playoff chances.

In a shocker in front of 57,659 fans, many of them Packers supporters who braved a strong winter storm to make it to Ford Field, the Detroit Lions knocked out the Packers' starting quarterback before halftime and used their third-string quarterback to eke out a win that snapped a streak of 19 straight NFC North division losses.

Even before Rodgers sustained his second concussion of the season -- he refused to slide at the end of an 18-yard scramble in the second quarter – the Packers appeared to lack the gumption necessary to beat the last-place Lions. With just two first downs and 68 net yards of offense in the first half, the Packers didn't come close to scoring.

Throw in three turnovers, including two while Rodgers was in the game, and the Packers were doomed.

Rodgers' backup, third-year pro Matt Flynn, led one scoring drive, a field goal that gave the Packers their only lead after the first series of the third quarter.

But with a chance to win the game with a fourth-quarter comeback, the Packers' drive stalled at the Lions' 31-yard line. Flynn had two possessions after the Lions went ahead 7-3 on a 13-yard screen pass for a touchdown from Drew Stanton to tight end Will Heller with 7:55 left. One of four sacks allowed by the Packers stalled the first drive, but the second one had real possibilities. ∎

OPPOSITE: Quarterback Aaron Rodgers hits his head on the turf as he's tackled by Lions linebacker Landon Johnson during the second quarter. Rodgers sustained a concussion on the play and did not return after this series. JULIAN H. GONZALEZ/DETROIT FREE PRESS

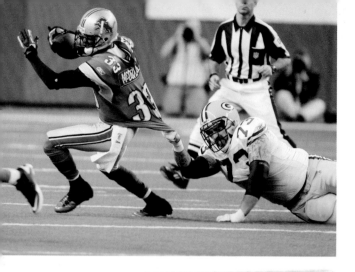

12.13.10 ★
WWW.PACKERSNEWS.COM
GREEN BAY PRESS-GAZETTE

PACKERS**FINAL**

 7   3 » Packers fall to 8-5 with Pats looming

MOTOR CITY HEADACHE

Packers quarterback Aaron Rodgers' head hits the turf as he's tackled by the Detroit Lions' Landon Johnson (55) and Amari Spievey in the second quarter of Sunday's game at Ford Field in Detroit. **Julian H. Gonzalez/Detroit Free Press**

Rodgers hurt, offense struggles in loss to Lions

BY ROB DEMOVSKY
rdemovsky@greenbaypressgazette.com

DETROIT — Aaron Rodgers took another blow to the head, and the Green Bay Packers took a blow to their ego, if not their playoff chances.

In a shocker in front of 57,659 fans, many of them Packers supporters who braved wintry conditions to make it to Ford Field, the Detroit Lions knocked out the Packers' starting quarterback before halftime and used their third-string tailback to eke out a 7-3 win that snapped a streak of 19 straight NFC North division losses.

Even before Rodgers sustained his second concussion of the season when he refused to slide at the end of an 18-yard scramble in the second quarter, the Packers appeared to lack the gumption necessary to beat the last-place Lions. Just two first downs and 68 total

AT PACKERSNEWS.COM

Get our complete online wrapup of Sunday's game, including:
■ **Photos** from the game
■ **Video:** Kareem Copeland's analysis of the game
■ **Pete Dougherty's** postgame chat with readers

Packers quarterback Matt Flynn reacts after throwing an incomplete pass in the fourth

where they may."

With three games remaining, the Packers sit at 8-5 heading into next Sunday night's road test against the New England Patriots, who have drilled their last two opponents (the New York Jets and the Chicago Bears) by a combined 81-10. Chicago's loss meant the Packers remained a game behind in the NFC North, but their stumble in the Motor City could hurt them in the tiebreaker scenarios. It was the Packers' second division loss,

in the stands ... so the atmosphere everything (was good). I didn't see any signs of this during the week of preparation. I thought the week of preparation was a good week. It wasn't a great week, but I thought they were definitely dialed in. I made a point of this type of game (Saturday) night in the team meeting. That's what's so frustrating to me, to come over here and the importance of a division game and to start the game way we did.

"We need to quit having these types of lessons, particularly this late in the year. But the positive part about it is everything that we still want to accomplish is in front of us."

It was a scoreless game when Rodgers took a combination hit from safety Amari Spievy and linebacker Landon Johnson late in the first half. Rodgers struggled to get to his feet and although he stayed in for three more plays, he was ruled out because of a

ABOVE: Running back Brandon Jackson is stopped for a loss in the backfield by Lions defensive tackle Ndamukong Suh. Guard Jason Spitz is at right. JULIAN H. GONZALEZ/DETROIT FREE PRESS

ABOVE: Running back Brandon Jackson is stopped for a loss in the backfield by Lions defensive tackle Ndamukong Suh. Guard Jason Spitz is at right. JULIAN H. GONZALEZ/DETROIT FREE PRESS

ABOVE LEFT: Left guard Daryn Colledge tackles Lions cornerback Dante Wesley after he recovered a fumble during the first quarter. JULIAN H. GONZALEZ/DETROIT FREE PRESS

ABOVE: Wide receiver Greg Jennings bobbles a pass that was intercepted Lions cornerback Amari Spievey, right, during the first quarter. KIRTHMON F. DOZIER/DETROIT FREE PRESS

LEFT: Lions fullback Jerome Felton is wrapped up by cornerback Charles Woodson (21) and linebackers Desmond Bishop (55) and A.J. Hawk (50) during the first quarter. Linebacker Clay Matthews (52) is at the top of the pile. KIRTHMON F. DOZIER/DETROIT FREE PRESS

BELOW: Running back Brandon Jackson is tackled by Lions cornerback Brandon McDonald during the second quarter. KIRTHMON F. DOZIER/DETROIT FREE PRESS

RIGHT: Right guard Josh Sitton, right, blocks Lions defensive tackle Ndamukong Suh during the second half. KIRTHMON F. DOZIER/DETROIT FREE PRESS

LEFT: Lions tight end Will Heller dives past cornerback Tramon Williams, top, and linebacker A.J. Hawk into the end zone on a 13-yard touchdown pass from quarterback Drew Stanton during the fourth quarter. It was the game's only touchdown, and the game-winner. JULIAN H. GONZALEZ/DETROIT FREE PRESS

BELOW LEFT: Lions running back Jahvid Best is tackled by cornerback Charles Woodson (21) and safety Charlie Peprah (26), who loses his helmet, during the fourth quarter. KIRTHMON F. DOZIER/DETROIT FREE PRESS

BELOW: Cornerback Tramon Williams pats Lions quarterback Drew Stanton on the helmet after the game. JULIAN H. GONZALEZ/DETROIT FREE PRESS

New England Patriots

December 19, 2010 • Gillette Stadium, Foxborough, Mass. • L 31-27

FOXBOROUGH, Mass. – Matt Flynn went toe-to-toe with the NFL's best player and one of its best teams, and took the Green Bay Packers to the brink of a major upset.

But in the end, New England quarterback Tom Brady, who six weeks later was named the NFL's most valuable player, got the touchdown he needed in the fourth quarter.

Flynn, the Packers' plucky backup quarterback starting in place of the concussed Aaron Rodgers, couldn't get the ball into the end zone in a chaotic final 30 seconds, taking a sack at the Patriots' 15-yard line on the final play.

Flynn, a third-year pro with minimal meaningful NFL playing time, did admirably in his first start. Statistically, he nearly matched Brady in passer rating (Brady's was 110.2 points, Flynn 100.2), threw for 251 yards to Brady's 163, and threw three touchdowns to Brady's two.

Flynn also had one costly play, an interception that Patriots safety Kyle Arrington returned 36 yards for a touchdown that put New England ahead 21-17 with 12:04 left in the third quarter.

Brady led a quick and efficient game-winning drive in the middle of the fourth quarter. ■

OPPOSITE: Linebacker Desmond Bishop celebrates after hitting Patriots quarterback Tom Brady during the second quarter. EVAN SIEGLE/PRESS-GAZETTE

ABOVE LEFT: Injured quarterback Aaron Rodgers watches from the sideline during the first quarter. Rodgers sat out the game with a concussion sustained the week before in Detroit. EVAN SIEGLE/PRESS-GAZETTE

ABOVE: Nick Collins (36) recovers an onside kick to start the game. Patriots cover man James Sanders is at left and the Packers' John Kuhn is at right. EVAN SIEGLE/PRESS-GAZETTE

LEFT: Collins celebrates after recovering the onside kick. EVAN SIEGLE/PRESS-GAZETTE

ABOVE RIGHT: Wide receiver James Jones runs down the sideline on a 66-yard touchdown pass in the second quarter. EVAN SIEGLE/PRESS-GAZETTE

BELOW RIGHT: Patriots safety Brandon Meriweather rides fullback John Kuhn to the ground near the goal line during the second quarter. EVAN SIEGLE/PRESS-GAZETTE

BELOW: Cornerback Sam Shields just misses an interception on a pass intended for Patriots wide receiver Brandon Tate during the first quarter. COREY WILSON/PRESS-GAZETTE

79

RIGHT: Linebacker Desmond Bishop, left, hits Patriots quarterback Tom Brady during the second quarter. EVAN SIEGLE/PRESS-GAZETTE

OPPOSITE: Nose tackle B.J. Raji sacks Patriots quarterback Tom Brady during the third quarter. EVAN SIEGLE/PRESS-GAZETTE

BELOW LEFT: Wide receiver Greg Jennings kneels in the end zone after scoring on a 1-yard pass during the second quarter. Running back Brandon Jackson is at right. EVAN SIEGLE/PRESS-GAZETTE

BELOW RIGHT: Coach Mike McCarthy looks at his play sheet during the second quarter. EVAN SIEGLE/PRESS-GAZETTE

ABOVE: Nose tackle B.J. Raji celebrates after sacking Patriots quarterback Tom Brady during the third quarter. EVAN SIEGLE/PRESS-GAZETTE

ABOVE RIGHT: Quarterback Matt Flynn (10) looks up at the scoreboard after the last play of the game. Patriots linebacker Dane Fletcher (52) is at upper right. EVAN SIEGLE/PRESS-GAZETTE

RIGHT: Quarterback Matt Flynn watches the ball bounce away after he was sacked by Patriots linebacker Tully Banta-Cain (95) on the last play of the game. EVAN SIEGLE/PRESS-GAZETTE

PACKERS FINAL

31 **27**

>> Flynn performs admirably in loss

NO TIME FOR MIRACLE

Green Bay Packers quarterback Matt Flynn reacts after the New England Patriots' Kyle Arrington returns an interception 36 yards for a touchdown in the third quarter Sunday at Gillette Stadium in Foxborough, Mass. **Evan Siegle/Press-Gazette**

Upset bid by Packers, Flynn can't overcome Pats

BY PETE DOUGHERTY
pdougher@greenbaypressgazette.com

FOXBOROUGH, Mass. — Matt Flynn went toe-to-toe with the NFL's best player and maybe best team, and took the Green Bay Packers to the brink of a major upset Sunday night.

But in the end, New England quarterback Tom Brady, the top candidate for this year's NFL most valuable play-

he had back, but I thought for his first start on a big stage against an excellent team he played very well and gave us a chance to win tonight."

Even with the loss, the 8-6 Packers came away Sunday with their playoff destiny in their control because of a fortuitous day for them in other games. With the New York Giants and Tampa Bay Buccaneers losing Sunday, the Packers are assured of qualifying for the playoffs by winning their last two

tiny, last two games at home. We're working and getting better. We like that."

Flynn, a third-year pro with minimal

AT PACKERSNEWS.COM

Get our complete online wrapup of Sunday's game, including:

- Photos from the game
- Video: Kareem Copeland's analysis
- Kareem's postgame chat with readers

England ahead 21-17 with 12:04 left in the third quarter. However, it's unclear how much of the responsibility Flynn should bear for the interception, because receiver James Jones stopped his out route, possibly bumped off by another defender before the throw.

Either way, Flynn recovered to put 10 more points on the board and give the Packers a 27-21 lead early in the fourth quarter. Then in the final 4:22, he got the ball back at the Packers' 43 and trailing by four, He moved the

ABOVE: Quarterback Matt Flynn walks off the field after the game. EVAN SIEGLE/PRESS-GAZETTE

New York Giants

December 26, 2010 • Lambeau Field, Green Bay • W 45-17

More than anything, the Green Bay Packers had to stand up to the New York Giants' brute physical force.

With the playoffs on the line, the Packers came through spectacularly.

They protected quarterback Aaron Rodgers with good pass blocking and play calling. They ran the ball well enough to keep the NFL's best front four honest. The neutralized the power run game that drives the Giants' offense.

All that helped magnify the difference in the team's quarterbacks, with the precise Rodgers embarrassing erratic Eli Manning in a blowout win that left the Packers in great shape to qualify for the playoffs.

Both teams came into this game needing a win to stay in the playoff hunt.

Giants halfbacks Brandon Jacobs and Ahmad Bradshaw rushed for a modest 78 yards on 20 carries, and each lost a critical fumble. Unable to run the ball like they did in their stunning NFC championship win on this same field in January 2008, the Giants relied on Manning, who couldn't keep the offense afloat. Manning, who led the league in interceptions coming into the game, threw four more – one each by Tramon Williams, Nick Collins, Sam Shields and A.J. Hawk. That was the game.

The difference between the two quarterbacks was startling. Rodgers, playing after missing a game because of a concussion, was as sharp as he'd been all season. He threw on the money (25-for-37), made plays in and out of the pocket (four touchdown passes, a career regular-season high 404 yards passing), and protected the ball (no interceptions). His passer rating of 139.9 points more than doubled Manning's 63.6. ■

OPPOSITE: Wide receiver Jordy Nelson points to the crowd as he scores on an 80-yard touchdown pass during the first quarter. Giants safety Deon Grant is at right. EVAN SIEGLE/PRESS-GAZETTE

ABOVE: Quarterback Aaron Rodgers makes the 'safe' sign after sliding feet-first for a first down during the first quarter of the game. Two weeks earlier, in Detroit, Rodgers sustained a concussion when he didn't slide on a scramble and he wound up missing the next game.
COREY WILSON/PRESS-GAZETTE

TOP: Quarterback Aaron Rodgers slides for a first down in front of Giants safety Deon Grant during the first quarter. COREY WILSON/PRESS-GAZETTE

RIGHT: Linebacker Clay Matthews hovers over Giants running back Brandon Jacobs after making a tackle during the first quarter. COREY WILSON/PRESS-GAZETTE

LEFT: This sign shows that Packers fans hadn't forgotten the 2007 NFC championship game, in which the Giants defeated the Packers at Lambeau Field. EVAN SIEGLE/PRESS-GAZETTE

BELOW LEFT: Linebacker Desmond Bishop (55) and a teammate tackle Giants running back Ahmad Bradshaw during the first quarter. EVAN SIEGLE/PRESS-GAZETTE

BELOW RIGHT: Cornerback Tramon Williams makes an interception in front of Giants wide receiver Hakeem Nicks during the first quarter. Linebacker Erik Walden is at right. EVAN SIEGLE/PRESS-GAZETTE

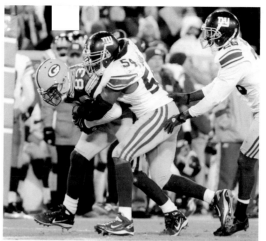

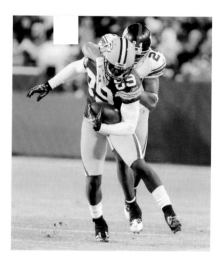

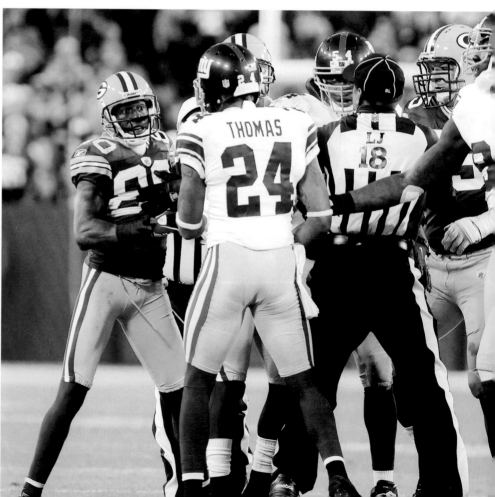

ABOVE: Linebacker Robert Francois puts a big hit on Giants quarterback Eli Manning during the second quarter. EVAN SIEGLE/PRESS-GAZETTE

ABOVE MIDDLE: Tight end Tom Crabtree, left, drags Giants linebacker Jonathan Goff for a first down during the third quarter. Giants safety Antrel Rolle is at right. COREY WILSON/PRESS-GAZETTE

ABOVE RIGHT: Wide receiver James Jones drags Giants cornerback Terrell Thomas for a first down during the third quarter. COREY WILSON/PRESS-GAZETTE

RIGHT: A scuffle ensues after wide receiver Donald Driver, left, was slapped in the helmet after being tackled by Giants cornerback Terrell Thomas during the second quarter. Thomas was called for a personal foul. COREY WILSON/PRESS-GAZETTE

OPPOSITE: Wide receiver Greg Jennings hauls in a 36-yard pass that gave the Packers a first down at the New York 1-yard line during the third quarter. Giants cornerback Corey Webster is at right. COREY WILSON/PRESS-GAZETTE

ABOVE: Tight end Donald Lee does a Lambeau Leap after scoring on a 1-yard touchdown pass during the third quarter. EVAN SIEGLE/PRESS-GAZETTE

OPPOSITE: Running back John Kuhn pounds over Giants linebacker Chase Blackburn and Packers tight end Tom Crabtree on a short touchdown run during the fourth quarter. COREY WILSON/PRESS-GAZETTE

12.27.10 ★
WWW.PACKERSNEWS.COM
GREEN BAY PRESS-GAZETTE

PACKERS FINAL

G **45** ny **17** » Packers are one win from playoffs

TAKING A GIANT STEP

Green Bay Packers nose tackle B.J. Raji (90) sacks New York Giants quarterback Eli Manning in the third quarter of Sunday's game at Lambeau Field. **Evan Siegle/Press-Gazette**

Packers win battle up front in dumping New York

BY PETE DOUGHERTY
pdougher@greenbaypressgazette.com

AT PACKERSNEWS.COM
Get our complete online wrapup of Sunday's game, including:
■ Photos from the game
■ Postgame analysis video
■ Postgame chat with readers

More than anything, the Green Bay Packers on Sunday had to stand up to the New York Giants' brute physical force.

And with the playoffs on the line, the Packers

"We knew this was going to be a battle that started up front," coach Mike McCarthy said, "and I don't need to see the film to say that we definitely commanded that battle."

Both teams came into this game needing a win to stay in the

feat New Orleans, because that three-way tiebreaker would go down to strength of victory, which the Packers have clinched. If they tie only with the Giants, the Packers are in because they won head-to-head, and if the

Chicago Bears

January 2, 2011 • Lambeau Field, Green Bay • W 10-3

The Green Bay Packers got in.

They got there with the greatest of difficulty, because the Chicago Bears were hell-bent on knocking their NFC North rivals from the playoffs. How else to explain Bears coach Lovie Smith staying with his starters the full 60 minutes even though his team was locked into the NFC's No. 2 seed before the game?

Smith's big swing didn't work, because Packers coach Mike McCarthy's team answered with one of its finest defensive performances of the season, including safety Nick Collins' interception in the final 20 seconds that clinched the Packers' win and a wild-card playoff berth.

Smith's approach was nothing short of shocking and one few NFL coaches would have taken in a game that meant nothing for his team in the standings.

The Packers didn't have much going most of the day and punted eight times in part because they couldn't run the ball against the NFL's third-ranked rush defense. Running backs James Starks, Brandon Jackson and John Kuhn combined for only 39 yards on 16 carries.

The Packers finally got their touchdown in the fourth quarter, set up by back-to-back completions of 21 yards to Donald Driver and 46 yards to Greg Jennings, the kind of shots that were the staple of the offense most of the season but were infrequent on this day.

That 10-3 lead held up over the final 12½ minutes because the Bears had even less going. Dom Capers, the Packers' defensive coordinator, played more of his base 3-4 defense in the second half to slow halfback Matt Forte, who had 54 yards on six carries in the first two quarters, but only 37 yards on nine carries thereafter. ■

OPPOSITE: Quarterback Aaron Rodgers circles the field, high-fiving fans after the game. COREY WILSON/PRESS-GAZETTE

ABOVE: Cornerback Charles Woodson (21) and linebackers Desmond Bishop (55) and A.J. Hawk (50) converge to stop Bears running back Matt Forte (22) during the first quarter. EVAN SIEGLE/PRESS-GAZETTE

ABOVE RIGHT: Linebacker Erik Walden (93) sacks Bears quarterback Jay Cutler during the third quarter. Linebacker Clay Matthews (52) also is in on the play. EVAN SIEGLE/PRESS-GAZETTE

RIGHT: Walden celebrates after sacking Cutler during the third quarter. Walden was picked up on waivers in midseason and became a key player down the stretch. EVAN SIEGLE/PRESS-GAZETTE

ABOVE: Cornerback Charles Woodson (21) sacks Bears quarterback Jay Cutler (6) during the fourth quarter. EVAN SIEGLE/PRESS-GAZETTE

LEFT: Nose tackle Howard Green, left, and linebacker Erik Walden sandwich Bears running back Matt Forte during the fourth quarter. COREY WILSON/PRESS-GAZETTE

BELOW: Linebacker Clay Matthews flexes after tackling Bears quarterback Jay Cutler during the fourth quarter. COREY WILSON/PRESS-GAZETTE

GREENBAYPRESSGAZETTE.COM

75¢

GREEN BAY PRESS-GAZETTE

WEATHER: CHANCE OF LIGHT SNOW HIGH 23, LOW 13 ★ **PAGE A-10**   **MONDAY,** JANUARY 3, 2011

Financial scams often target the elderly

Senior citizens lose $2.6B annually, study says

BY KIMBALL PERRY
The Cincinnati Enquirer
AND STEVE CONTORNO
scontorno@greenbaypressgazette.com

A seemingly desperate phone call from a grandson stuck overseas is hardly ever what it seems to be.

In fact, more often than not, it's a scam aimed at Grandma and Grandpa in hopes they'll unknowingly wire thousands of dollars in haste.

More than 1 million senior citizens lose $2.6 billion per year on scams or other forms of financial exploitation, according to a study last year by the MetLife Mature Market Institute. About 60 percent of that loss came at the hands of the victims' family members, the study estimates.

"It is a significant issue, one that we're always looking to address and stay ahead of," said Lee Sensenbrenner, spokesperson for the Wisconsin Department of Agriculture, Trade and Consumer Protection.

"What we advise, in the case of the grandparents scam, is always try to confirm whatever anyone is telling you, whether it's over the phone or through an email. Try to verify it independently."

Many cases go unreported because elderly victims don't want to deal with the shame or other ramifications — loss of independence, loss of control over finances, fear of being placed in a nursing home — that can come with being victimized.

In Wisconsin, victims of scams and consumer fraud aren't required to give their age when they report a scam, so the number of seniors targeted each year is not documented. But it is prevalent.

"When we know there's something happening in the community, we try to print up a warning and send it out to folks who we speak with all the time," said Sunny Archambault, director of the Aging & Disability Resource Center of Brown County.

Those closest to the elderly actually can be the biggest abusers.

"Research indicates that adult children are the most frequent abusers," said Laurie Petrie, spokeswoman for the Council on Aging of Southwest Ohio.

➤ See Scams, A-2

MORE DETAILS

You can reach the Wisconsin Department of Agriculture, Trade and Consumer Protection online at http://datcp.wi.gov/ or by calling the consumer protection hot line at (800) 422-7128

PLAYOFF BOUND!

Green Bay Packers safety Nick Collins turns toward the crowd following his game-clinching interception against the Chicago Bears during the fourth quarter of the game Sunday at Lambeau Field in Green Bay. **Corey Wilson/Press-Gazette**

Packers defeat Bears 10-3, will play Eagles on Sunday

Green Bay Packers quarterback Aaron Rodgers gives high-fives to fans Sunday after the Packers defeated the Chicago Bears. **Evan Siegle/Press-Gazette**

On to Philadelphia!

The chorus is not original, because that anthem was blazoned across the front page of the Green Bay Press-Gazette 50 years ago when the Packers won their way into the National Football League championship game.

But Sunday's gasping 10-3 victory over the Chicago Bears at Lambeau Field gives fans a chance to revive the chant, and their team the right to retain Super Bowl visions with 11 other teams.

TONY WALTER
Commentary

➤ See Bound, A-2

Walker hopes for fast start as governor

Legislature called into special session

BY SCOTT BAUER
The Associated Press

MADISON — In his first day as governor, Scott

➤ Johnson set to begin new life, as

Walker

have 250,000 more jobs than it does now.

Wisconsin is showing signs of recovering from the recession that resulted in a loss of 180,000 jobs the past

calling the special session and he's worked behind the scenes with Republican legislative leaders on a series of measures he wants them to take up right out of the gate.

Those include revamping the state Commerce Department into a public-private hybrid that's more focused

agencies, a move Democrats derided as nothing more than a power grab and unnecessary given that Walker appointees who head the agencies are making the proposals.

Walker defends it as a way to create more accountability and remove the ability of bureaucrats to make far-reaching rules and regula-

NEWS NATION

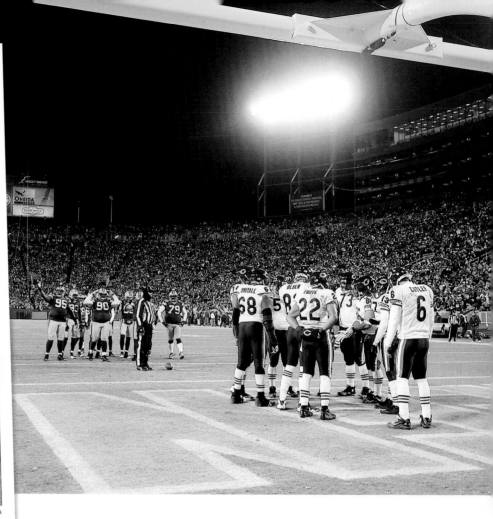

ABOVE: The Packers' defense waits for the Bears to start their final drive from the Chicago 3-yard line during the fourth quarter. EVAN SIEGLE/PRESS-GAZETTE

ABOVE: Quarterback Aaron Rodgers high-fives fans as he runs around the field after the game. EVAN SIEGLE/PRESS-GAZETTE

ABOVE LEFT: Wide receiver Donald Driver high-fives fans as he runs around the field after the game. EVAN SIEGLE/PRESS-GAZETTE

LEFT: Tight end Donald Lee (86) is congratulated by teammate Jordy Nelson after Lee caught a 1-yard touchdown pass during the fourth quarter. It turned out to be the game-winner. EVAN SIEGLE/PRESS-GAZETTE

Philadelphia Eagles

January 9, 2011 • Lincoln Financial Field, Philadelphia • W 21-16

PHILADELPHIA – If nothing else, the first round of the NFL playoffs revealed the stark difference between the Green Bay Packers of the 2009 season and the Packers of 2010.

In 2009, their defense hemorrhaged against first-rate quarterbacks, including giving up 379 yards passing and five touchdown passes to Kurt Warner in an overtime loss in a wild-card game at Arizona.

This year? Different story.

The always-frightening Michael Vick came in at the helm of a Philadelphia Eagles offense that was among the NFL's best. But unlike the previous year, the Packers moved on to the divisional round of the postseason because they had the goods to deal with an explosive offense that ranked No. 2 in the league in yards and No. 2 in points.

With the right mix of playmakers, blitzes, coverages and spies, the Packers kept Vick from taking control of the game. Tramon Williams made the clinching interception in the end zone with 33 seconds to play.

The Packers sacked Vick three times and held him to a passer rating of only 79.9 points, a full 20 points less than his regular-season rating of 100.2 points, which was fourth-best in the NFL. He also gained only 33 yards on eight runs, with a long scramble of 14 yards. That counts as an excellent day against a quarterback who can dominate games with his running.

While Vick was only able to flash his abilities, his counterpart, Packers quarterback Aaron Rodgers, played a steady, mistake-free game. ■

OPPOSITE: Running back James Starks is tackled by Eagles safety Kurt Coleman (42) as defensive end Trent Cole (58) closes in.
EVAN SIEGLE/PRESS-GAZETTE

ABOVE: Tight end Tom Crabtree scores on a 7-yard touchdown pass during the first quarter. Eagles cornerback Asante Samuel is at right. COREY WILSON/PRESS-GAZETTE

RIGHT: Linebacker Desmond Bishop sacks Eagles quarterback Michael Vick during the first quarter. COREY WILSON/PRESS-GAZETTE

FAR RIGHT: Cornerback Sam Shields breaks up a pass intended for Eagles receiver Jeremy Maclin. EVAN SIEGLE/PRESS-GAZETTE

RIGHT: Linebacker Erik Walden tackles Eagles quarterback Michael Vick during the first quarter. EVAN SIEGLE/PRESS-GAZETTE

BELOW RIGHT: Wide receiver James Jones spikes the ball after scoring on a 9-yard touchdown pass during the second quarter. EVAN SIEGLE/PRESS-GAZETTE

BELOW: Running back James Starks breaks into the secondary during the first quarter. Eagles cornerback Dimitri Patterson is at left. COREY WILSON/PRESS-GAZETTE

ABOVE: Linebacker Clay Matthews swoops into the backfield to sack Eagles quarterback Michael Vick during the second quarter. EVAN SIEGLE/PRESS-GAZETTE

RIGHT: Linebacker Clay Matthews sacks Eagles quarterback Michael Vick during the second quarter. EVAN SIEGLE/PRESS-GAZETTE

ABOVE: Wide receiver James Jones drops a pass against Eagles cornerback Asante Samuel during the second quarter. EVAN SIEGLE/PRESS-GAZETTE

LEFT: Linebacker Clay Matthews sacks Eagles quarterback Michael Vick during the second quarter. COREY WILSON/PRESS-GAZETTE

PACKERS FINAL

G 21 **E** 16 » Packers advance to face the Falcons

DEFENSE IS DIFFERENCE

Green Bay Packers linebacker Clay Matthews hits Philadelphia Eagles quarterback Michael Vick for a sack during the second quarter of Sunday's wild-card playoff game at Lincoln Financial Field in Philadelphia. **Corey Wilson/Press-Gazette**

Packers hold down Vick, hang on to top Eagles

BY PETE DOUGHERTY
pdougher@greenbaypressgazette.com

PHILADELPHIA — If nothing else, the first round of the NFL playoffs revealed the stark difference between the Green Bay Packers of last season and this season's team.

A year ago, their defense hemorrhaged against first-rate quarterbacks, including giving up 379 yards passing and five touchdown passes to Kurt Warner in an overtime loss of a wild-card game at Arizona. This year? Different story.

The always frightening Michael Vick came into Sunday at the helm of a Philadelphia Eagles offense that is among the NFL's best. But unlike a year ago, the Packers are moving on to the divisional round of the postseason because they had the goods to deal with an explosive offense that ranked No. 2 in the league in yards and No. 2 in points.

With the right mix of playmakers,

UP NEXT
■ **Saturday:** Packers at Atlanta, 7 p.m. (WLUK, Channel 11)

AT PACKERSNEWS.COM
■ Video interviews with Packers players about the game.
■ Photo gallery from Sunday's game.
■ Photos from the 2004 playoff loss to the Philadelphia Eagles, aka "the fourth-and-26 game."

blitzes, coverages and spies, the Packers kept Vick from taking control of the game then made the clinching interception in the end zone with 33 seconds to play in their 21-16 win at Lincoln Financial Field.

"It's tough for teams to score on us, I don't care who they are," defensive end Ryan Pickett said. "Vick is probably the worst — we're so happy to have that behind, he's such a headache to prepare for because he can throw it and run it. We do a good job keeping people out of the end zone. I think we're much better this year."

The win means the sixth-seeded Packers (10-6) will play at top-seeded Atlanta (13-3) on Saturday night in an NFC divisional-round rematch of a game earlier this season that the Falcons won 20-17 at the Georgia Dome. The winner advances to the NFC championship against the winner of the conference's other divisional-round game, Chicago vs. Seattle.

The Falcons are a daunting 20-2 at the Georgia Dome in games started by their fine young quarterback, Matt Ryan.

"We feel like we left a lot of football out on the field in that (first Atlanta) game," cornerback Charles Woodson said. "We had points defensively where we could have gotten off the field, third-down situations, missed tackles — our tackling was probably the poorest we've been all season. We don't fore-

see that happening again. We look forward to going down there."

To get there, the Packers' charge Sunday was to make Vick a pocket passer, at least as much as is possible against the game's premier scrambler. Though Vick has been a much more accurate passer in his second incarnation in the NFL, he's still at his most dangerous when he's gashing a defense with a big scramble on one play, then breaking out of the pocket and throwing a dart down field to his explosive receivers (DeSean Jackson and Jeremy Maclin) or tight end (Brent Celek) on the next.

A big part of defensive coordinator Dom Capers' plan was for the pass rushers to hold their lanes whether it was a conventional four-man rush, or a five- or six-man blitz, and sacrifice possible sacks to prevent Vick from getting outside the pocket. And the Packers did all they could to push the

► Packers, Page 6

LEFT: Running back Brandon Jackson raises the ball as he runs into the end zone on a 16-yard touchdown pass during the third quarter. Eagles cornerback Josello Hanson (21) is at left. EVAN SIEGLE/PRESS-GAZETTE

BELOW: Safety Nick Collins celebrates after making a tackle during the third quarter. EVAN SIEGLE/PRESS-GAZETTE

ABOVE: The offensive line dominated the Eagles' defensive line. From left, right tackle Bryan Bulaga (75) pushes down defensive end Darryl Tapp (91) as right guard Josh Sitton (71), right, fends off defensive end Trent Cole during the fourth quarter. COREY WILSON/PRESS-GAZETTE

RIGHT: Eagles kicker David Akers (2) is dismayed after missing a 34-yard field-goal try during the fourth quarter. He also missed from 41 yards in the first quarter. After the game, Eagles safety Quintin Mikell said Akers had been distracted by an off-the-field matter. Three weeks later, Akers told the Philadelphia Inquirer that his 6-year-old daughter had undergone cancer surgery in the week before the Eagles played the Packers. COREY WILSON/PRESS-GAZETTE

OPPOSITE LEFT: Cornerback Tramon Williams intercepts a pass intended for Eagles wide receiver Riley Cooper during the fourth quarter. The interception clinched the victory. EVAN SIEGLE/PRESS-GAZETTE

OPPOSITE RIGHT: Cornerback Tramon Williams (on bottom) is mobbed by linebacker Erik Walden (93), safety Nick Collins (36) and other teammates after his game-clinching interception in the fourth quarter. EVAN SIEGLE/PRESS-GAZETTE

GREENBAYPRESSGAZETTE.COM

75¢

GREEN BAY PRESS-GAZETTE

MONDAY, JANUARY 10, 2011

PACKERS PUSH ON TO ATLANTA

Green Bay Packers linebacker Erik Walden tackles Philadelphia Eagles quarterback Michael Vick in the first quarter of Sunday's wild-card round game at Lincoln Financial Field in Philadelphia.
Evan Siegle/Press-Gazette

Fans primed for the next playoff stop after Green Bay's 21-16 win over Eagles

BY PATTI ZARLING

phia. The Packers will face the At-

Schmidt said. "I think Philadel-

PLAYOFFS
DIVISIONAL ROUND

SHARE YOUR THOUGHTS
What do the Packers have to do next Saturday

Atlanta Falcons

January 15, 2011 • Georgia Dome, Atlanta • W 48-21

ATLANTA – Aaron Rodgers, Tramon Williams and the rest of the Green Bay Packers stormed into the rowdy Georgia Dome and gave the NFC's top-seeded Atlanta Falcons a brutal playoff whuppin'.

The white-hot Rodgers blistered Atlanta's defense on drive after drive with playmaking scrambles and pinpoint passing. Williams made two game-turning plays late in the second quarter to propel the Packers to a convincing win.

The Packers' dominance against the Falcons was so complete that even two huge errors in the first half – receiver Greg Jennings' lost fumble on the team's first possession, and the 102-yard kickoff return they allowed to Eric Weems that put Atlanta ahead 14-7 early in the second quarter – could only momentarily slow the onslaught.

The difference in yards (442 for the Packers, 194 for the Falcons) and turnovers (one for the Packers, four for the Falcons) better reflected the difference between these teams on this day than the score, bad enough as that was.

Rodgers' game was one for the ages: He completed 31 of 36 passes for 366 yards and a passer rating of 136.8 points, his second-best rating of the season. Considering what was on the line, it may have been the best game of his career.

With no run game to balance Atlanta's offense – halfback Michael Turner had only 10 carries for 39 yards because the Falcons were in catch-up mode most of the game – quarterback Matt Ryan couldn't carry his team like Rodgers did his, finishing with a 71.4 passer rating and 186 passing yards. ■

OPPOSITE: Cornerback Tramon Williams celebrates after returning an interception 70 yards for a touchdown at the end of the second quarter. Safety Charlie Peprah (26) is at right. EVAN SIEGLE/PRESS-GAZETTE

ABOVE: From left, linebacker Clay Matthews (52), defensive end Cullen Jenkins (77) and cornerback Charles Woodson (21) pressure Falcons quarterback Matt Ryan during the first quarter. Matthews sacked Ryan on the play. EVAN SIEGLE/PRESS-GAZETTE

ABOVE: Falcons quarterback Matt Ryan (2), caught between guard Justin Blalock (63) and center Todd McClure (62), fumbles during the fourth quarter. Packers linebacker Clay Matthews recovered the ball. Falcons guard Harvey Dahl (73) is at right. EVAN SIEGLE/PRESS-GAZETTE

LEFT: Defensive end Cullen Jenkins celebrates after making a tackle during the first quarter. EVAN SIEGLE/PRESS-GAZETTE

BELOW: Packers fan Angela Berger of Atlanta is all smiles as she tailgates outside the Georgia Dome before the game. EVAN SIEGLE/PRESS-GAZETTE

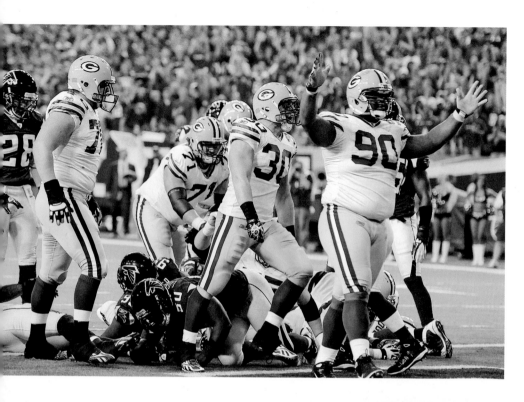

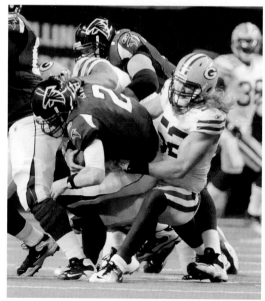

ABOVE: Nose tackle B.J. Raji (90) cheers a 1-yard touchdown run by fullback John Kuhn (30) during the second quarter. Raji was used as a blocking back on the play. COREY WILSON/PRESS-GAZETTE

RIGHT: Linebacker Clay Matthews sacks Falcons quarterback Matt Ryan during the second quarter. COREY WILSON/PRESS-GAZETTE

FAR RIGHT: Wide receiver James Jones outjumps Falcons cornerback Brent Grimes to haul in a 20-yard touchdown pass during the second quarter. COREY WILSON/PRESS-GAZETTE

ABOVE: Cornerback Tramon Williams intercepts a pass intended for Falcons receiver Michael Jenkins in the end zone during the second quarter. COREY WILSON/PRESS-GAZETTE

RIGHT: Cornerback Tramon Williams returns an interception 70 yards for a touchdown at the end of the second quarter. Falcons guard Harvey Dahl gives chase. COREY WILSON/PRESS-GAZETTE

ABOVE LEFT: Quarterback Aaron Rodgers evades the diving tackle attempt of Falcons linebacker Curtis Lofton on a 7-yard touchdown run during the third quarter.
EVAN SIEGLE/PRESS-GAZETTE

LEFT: Quarterback Aaron Rodgers scrambles and throws on the run during the third quarter. EVAN SIEGLE/PRESS-GAZETTE

ABOVE: Cornerback Charles Woodson pressures Falcons quarterback Matt Ryan as he throws to wide receiver Brian Finneran (86) during the third quarter. COREY WILSON/PRESS-GAZETTE

LEFT: Running back James Starks goes over the top of Falcons linebackers Curtis Lofton (50) and Coy Wire (52) during the third quarter. COREY WILSON/PRESS-GAZETTE

ABOVE: Fullback John Kuhn flies through the air as he scores a touchdown against Falcons linebacker Curtis Lofton during the third quarter. Kuhn caught a 7-yard pass from quarterback Aaron Rodgers. EVAN SIEGLE/PRESS-GAZETTE

GREENBAYPRESSGAZETTE.COM

GREEN BAY PRESS-GAZETTE

WEATHER: MOSTLY CLOUDY HIGH 13, LOW 7 ★ **PAGE B-9** | $625 worth of coupons in today's paper | **SUNDAY,** JANUARY 16, 2011

PACKERS 48 Ⓖ FALCONS 21

STUNNER

Packers pick apart top-seeded Falcons, advance to NFC championship game

Green Bay Packers cornerback Tramon Williams returns an interception for a touchdown as Falcons guard Harvey Dahl pursues on Saturday at the Georgia Dome. ers up 28-14 at halftime as they stunned the Falcons 48-21 to advance to the Jan. 23 NFC championship game. **Corey Wilson/Press-Gazette**

Go ahead, Green Bay. Smile, honk your horn, raise a glass or two.

The NFC championship game will include the Green Bay Packers for the second time in the past four seasons and the fifth time in the past 16. That's celebration material on any cold Wisconsin day.

TONY WALTER
twalter@greenbay pressgazette.com

The evidence was conclusive Saturday night with a 48-21 dismantling of the top-seeded Atlanta Falcons, which sends the Packers into the Jan. 23 Super Bowl play-in game against either the Chicago Bears or Seattle Seahawks.

➤ See Stunner, A-2

PACKERS INS...
For complete coverage of Saturd... see the **PACKERS FINAL SECTIO**

PACKERS ON...
In addition, go to www.Packers...
of the playoffs, including:
➤ Stories and analysis about th...
➤ Videos and photo galleries fro...
➤ Fan features
➤ Submit your fan photos

INSIDE: CLASSIFIEDS ■ E-1 | **LOTTERIES** ■ A-4 | **NATION/WORLD** ■ B-6
OBITUARIES ■ B-8 | **PUZZLES** ■ E-4, E-5 | **TV** ■ INSERT

CONTACT US: Newsroom (920) 431-8400 | Subscription/Delivery/Payment (877) 424-5042 | Advertising (920) 431-8300
Online (920) 431-8211 ● Copyright 2011 | Green Bay Press-Gazette | A Gannett newspaper

1.16.11 ★
WWW.PACKERSNEWS.COM
GREEN BAY **PRESS-GAZETTE**

PACKERS **FINAL**

Ⓖ 48 Falcons 21 » Packers move to NFC title game

ATLANTA THRASHING

Quarterback Aaron Rodgers celebrates as time expires in the Green Bay Packers' 48-21 victory over the Atlanta Falcons in an NFC divisional round playoff game on Saturday at the Georgia Dome in Atlanta. **Evan Siegle/Press-Gazette**

Packers' confidence soars after stomping Falcons

BY PETE DOUGHERTY
pdougher@greenbaypressgazette.com

ATLANTA — Aaron Rodgers, Tramon Williams and the rest of Green Bay Packers stormed into the rowdy Georgia Dome on Saturday night and gave the NFC's top-seeded Atlanta Falcons a brutal playoff whuppin'.

The white-hot Rodgers blistered Atlanta's defense drive after drive with playmaking scrambles and pinpoint pass...

AT PACKERSNEWS.COM
Video: The PackersNews.com reporting team analyzes Saturday's game. In addition, check out more wrap-ups on the game, including:
■ Video interviews with Packers players about the game.
■ Photos, video
■ Text GPGPACKERS to 4info (44636) to have alerts sent to your mobile device.

...ed but ultra-confident Packers.
"We're a championship-caliber football team," coach Mike McCarthy said. "We talked about it before the...

these teams on this day than the score, bad enough as that was.

It started with Rodgers, who in back-to-back games...

ABOVE: Linebacker Clay Matthews raises his hands in victory as he leaves the field after the game. COREY WILSON/PRESS-GAZETTE

Chicago Bears

January 23, 2011 • Soldier Field, Chicago • W 21-14

CHICAGO — Fittingly and deservingly, the Green Bay Packers made it back to the Super Bowl by outlasting their oldest and most stubborn opponent, the Chicago Bears, in the NFC championship game at Soldier Field.

It was what the Packers' legions of fans had long dreamed about.

Nothing but joy spilled from the Packers' locker room after the game.

After the accepting the George Halas Trophy as the NFC champion, Packers president and CEO Mark Murphy said this experience was better than when he first played in a Super Bowl with the Washington Redskins in the strike-shortened 1982 season.

"Now I want to win a ring as Packers president," Murphy said.

Retired team president Bob Harlan said the Super Bowl trip was a defining moment for this generation of Packers players and fans.

"We went with Ron Wolf and Mike Holmgren and now we're going with Ted Thompson and Mike McCarthy," Harlan said. "They've done it."

Quarterback Aaron Rodgers was the center of attention, naturally.

"This is what I've dreamed about since I was a kid growing up in northern California and watching (San Francisco 49ers quarterback) Joe Montana," Rodgers said.

For all the excitement, some unfinished business remained.

"People play for years and years and never make it to the Super Bowl. Let alone go and win it. So, that's the goal," safety Charlie Peprah said. "I don't want to take this opportunity for granted. We've been counting down the quarters. We've got four more quarters to go."

From the start of a clear, cold Sunday, the Packers showed why they were 3½-point favorites even though they were seeded lower than the Bears and playing on the road.

The Packers jumped out a 14-0 halftime lead on short runs by Rodgers and rookie running back James Starks but didn't do much else on offense. They survived the Bears' shocking rally and moved on to the Super Bowl mostly on the back of a defense that had become one of the NFL's best.

The Bears had basically nothing going for the first three quarters, in which they were shut out. After quarterback Jay Cutler left the game after the first series of the third quarter because of a knee injury, the Bears appeared to have no chance.

But a plucky defense and third-string quarterback Caleb Hanie's ability to engineer two touchdown drives in the fourth quarter got the Bears back in it.

Down the stretch, three players delivered big plays for the Packers.

On the first drive of the second half, with the Packers in the red zone with a chance to go ahead by three touchdowns, Rodgers threw an interception right to Bears linebacker Brian Urlacher. Just when it seemed Urlacher would return it for a touchdown, Rodgers tripped him up at the Bears' 45-yard line. Chicago couldn't convert the turnover into points, so the Packers' two-touchdown lead held.

"I don't get paid to tackle, but that was probably one of my better plays of the day," Rodgers said.

B.J. Raji, the 337-pound nose tackle, dropped back in coverage in the fourth quarter, picked off Hanie's pass and returned it 18 yards for a touchdown. It put the Packers ahead 21-7 and proved to be the difference in the game after Hanie led the Bears to another score.

At the end, it was cornerback Sam Shields, an undrafted rookie who had the game of his career with two interceptions. The first was a leaping catch at the Packers' 3 late in the first half. The other was the clincher, on fourth-and-5 at the Packers' 12, thwarting Hanie's last-ditch attempt to tie the game in the final minute. ■

OPPOSITE: Cornerback Sam Shields sacks Bears quarterback Jay Cutler during the second quarter. It was believed to have been the play on which Cutler injured his left knee. EVAN SIEGLE/PRESS-GAZETTE

RIGHT: Nick Lucas of Green Bay celebrates a big play while watching the game at Swobey's Hideout on Green Bay's east side. MATTHEW L. BECKER

BOTTOM RIGHT: Craig Stillman of Green Bay sports a Clay Matthews-style wig while tailgating at Soldier Field before the game. COREY WILSON/PRESS-GAZETTE

BELOW: Derek Carroll of San Antonio, Texas, is decked out in green and gold as he wears his cheesehead and a bandanna while standing outside Soldier Field before the game. It was 20 degrees and sunny at kickoff. EVAN SIEGLE/PRESS-GAZETTE

ABOVE: Quarterback Aaron Rodgers throws downfield during the first quarter. At right, center Scott Wells (63) blocks Bears nose tackle Anthony Adams. COREY WILSON/PRESS-GAZETTE

ABOVE RIGHT: Quarterback Aaron Rodgers looks to pass during the first quarter under pressure from Bears defensive tackle Matt Toeaina (75). At right, left tackle Chad Clifton (76) keeps Bears defensive end Julius Peppers (90) at bay. The Packers' offense struggled when Clifton missed three series with a stringer, but he returned to the game. COREY WILSON/PRESS-GAZETTE

RIGHT: Quarterback Aaron Rodgers heads off the field after scoring on a 1-yard touchdown during the first quarter. EVAN SIEGLE/PRESS-GAZETTE

ABOVE: Defensive end Cullen Jenkins hangs on to the legs of Bears running back Matt Forte as linebacker Clay Matthews comes into help during the first quarter. EVAN SIEGLE/PRESS-GAZETTE

RIGHT: Tim Masthay punts to the Bears during the second quarter. His eight punts, and the coverage provided by the punt team, kept the Bears pinned in their territory throughout the game. Masthay landed five punts inside the Bears' 20-yard line. COREY WILSON/PRESS-GAZETTE

TOP RIGHT: Cover men Brett Swain (16) and Jarrett Bush (24 on ground) converge on Bears kick returner Danieal Manning (38) during the second quarter. Special teams played a big role in the Packers' victory, shutting down Manning and punt returner Devin Hester. COREY WILSON/PRESS-GAZETTE

BOTTOM RIGHT: Defensive end Cullen Jenkins celebrates a sack of Bears quarterback Jay Cutler during the first quarter. EVAN SIEGLE/PRESS-GAZETTE

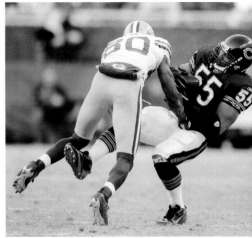

ABOVE: Bears linebacker Lance Briggs intercepts a pass that had bounced off wide receiver Donald Driver during the second quarter. EVAN SIEGLE/PRESS-GAZETTE

LEFT: Linebacker Desmond Bishop (55) and cornerback Sam Shields (37) hit Bears quarterback Jay Cutler, forcing a fumble during the second quarter. Bears running back Matt Forte recovered the fumble. COREY WILSON/PRESS-GAZETTE

ABOVE: Running back James Starks scores on a 4-yard touchdown run during the second quarter. COREY WILSON/PRESS-GAZETTE

LEFT: Quarterback Aaron Rodgers outruns Bears defensive tackle Tommie Harris (91) and llnebacker Brian Urlacher (54) as he scrambles to the sideline during the second quarter. COREY WILSON/PRESS-GAZETTE

OPPOSITE: Bears quarterback Jay Cutler hangs his head during the second quarter. He left the game early in the third quarter with a knee injury. COREY WILSON/PRESS-GAZETTE

BELOW: Quarterback Aaron Rodgers raises his arms to celebrate James Starks' 4-yard touchdown run during the second quarter. EVAN SIEGLE/PRESS-GAZETTE

RIGHT: Wide receiver Greg Jennings makes a catch against Bears linebacker Brian Urlacher during the third quarter. Jennings had eight catches for 130 yards. EVAN SIEGLE/PRESS-GAZETTE

LEFT: From upper left, linebacker A.J. Hawk, nose tackle B.J.Raji and defensive end Ryan Pickett wrap up Bears running back Matt Forte during the third quarter. EVAN SIEGLE/PRESS-GAZETTE

ABOVE: Cornerback Charles Woodson celebrates a defensive play during the third quarter. EVAN SIEGLE/PRESS-GAZETTE

RIGHT: Linebacker A.J. Hawk (50) and nose tackle B.J. Raji (90) pressure Bears quarterback Caleb Hanie during the fourth quarter. Hanie, the Bears' third-string quarterback, came into the game after starter Jay Cutler was injured and backup Todd Collins was ineffective. EVAN SIEGLE/PRESS-GAZETTE

LEFT: Nose tackle B.J. Raji returns an interception 18 yards for a touchdown during the fourth quarter. Bears backup quarterback Caleb Hanie, who threw the pass, tries to tackle him. COREY WILSON/PRESS-GAZETTE

BOTTOM LEFT: Raji gestures to the crowd after scoring on his interception. EVAN SIEGLE/PRESS-GAZETTE

BOTTOM RIGHT: Cornerback Sam Shields jumps on Raji's back to celebrate his touchdown. COREY WILSON/PRESS-GAZETTE

1.24.11 ★
WWW.**PACKERS**NEWS.COM
GREEN BAY **PRESS-GAZETTE**

PACKERS**FINAL**

21 14 » Packers whip Bears to win NFC title

BIG D

DEFENSE PAVES GREEN BAY'S ROAD TO SUPER BOWL XLV

OPPOSITE LEFT: Cornerback Sam Shields (37) makes a game-clinching interception against Bears receiver Johnny Knox (13) during the fourth quarter. EVAN SIEGLE/PRESS-GAZETTE

OPPOSITE RIGHT: Cornerback Sam Shields (37) is all smiles while being mobbed by his teammates, including safety Charlie Peprah (26) after making the game-clinching interception late in the fourth quarter. Bears running back Matt Forte (22) is at upper right. EVAN SIEGLE/PRESS-GAZETTE

ABOVE: Quarterback Aaron Rodgers raises his arms in victory as he leaves the field after the game. COREY WILSON/PRESS-GAZETTE

ABOVE: Wide receiver Donald Driver celebrates with Matt Klein, the Packers' football administration coordinator, after the game. EVAN SIEGLE/PRESS-GAZETTE

ABOVE: Joel and Kathy Swedberg of Appleton chant 'Go, Pack, go' as they wait for the Packers to arrive at Austin Straubel International Airport in Ashwaubenon after the game.
MATTHEW L. BECKER

RIGHT: A fan holds up the Green Bay Press-Gazette's extra section as she waits to welcome the Packers home at Austin Straubel International Airport in Ashwaubenon after the game.
MATTHEW L. BECKER

EXTRA! EXTRA! $1

GREEN BAY PRESS-GAZETTE

GREENBAYPRESSGAZETTE.COM   SUNDAY, JANUARY 23, 2011   PACKERSNEWS.COM

CHAMPS

PACKERS WIN NFC TITLE

Green Bay Packers Cullen Jenkins celebrates a sack of Chicago Bears quarterback Jay Cutler during the NFC championship game Sunday at Soldier Field in Chicago. Evan Siegle/Press-Gazette

INSIDE: RECAP OF PACKERS' ROAD TO SUPER BOWL XLV

Copyright 2011 | Green Bay Press-Gazette | A Gannett newspaper   CONTACT US:

Pittsburgh Steelers

February 6, 2011 • Cowboys Stadium, Arlington, Texas • W 31-25

ARLINGTON, Texas — The Vince Lombardi Trophy, named after the legendary Green Bay Packers coach, has returned to its rightful place after 14 long years.

It was an arduous journey for the Packers, who defeated the Pittsburgh Steelers in Super Bowl XLV to win their 13th championship – no NFL team has more – and their fourth Super Bowl title.

It was only fitting that this resilient group, which had overcome so much adversity over the course of the season, would need to dig deep one more time.

When veterans Charles Woodson and Donald Driver went down with injuries in the first half and couldn't return, and when the Steelers cut an 18-point deficit to three points midway through the fourth quarter, this Packers team did what it had done best all season.

It never wavered. It never lost confidence. It never took its eyes off the ultimate prize.

This was a team on a mission, and nothing would keep these Packers from their goal. No opponent and no twist of fate was going to deny them what they believed was theirs.

"You fight all season, a lot of things go on, it's all for this moment," Woodson said, beaming as he held the Lombardi Trophy. "There are no games next week, there's not another game in two weeks. This is it, and the last team standing is the Green Bay Packers. It's everything I wanted it to be."

Inside the locker room with Woodson were icons from the Packers' glorious past, including Bart Starr, Ron Wolf and Bob Harlan. Part of a family that seemingly passes its traditions from one generation to the next, they also expressed pride in the latest championship.

While there's no way to quantify or compare titles, what the 2010 Packers achieved could be the most impressive performance in the team's long history.

This Green Bay team didn't have the best record or the most victories. But no championship team in the Packers' storied past likely endured as much hardship, or bounced back from so many setbacks.

Six starters were lost during the course of the season and 15 players landed on season-ending injured reserve. They weathered six losses by four or fewer points. They didn't win the NFC North Division. They struggled to qualify for the last NFC playoff berth. They withstood a difficult three-game road playoff gauntlet just to make it to the Super Bowl.

So when adversity struck again in the Super Bowl, the Packers seemed ready for anything.

During an emotional halftime, Woodson tried to offer some motivation but broke down in tears. Driver stepped up and implored his teammates to go out and claim the Lombardi Trophy. There was no way these Packers, who had been through so much, were going to let their injured comrades or themselves down.

This championship also was about validation for general manager Ted Thompson and coach Mike McCarthy, who were harshly criticized in some corners when they handed the starting quarterback job to Aaron Rodgers in 2008.

The Packers' leaders stuck to their convictions and were rewarded for their vision and their principles. This Super Bowl triumph and Rodgers' MVP performance – he threw for 304 yards and three touchdowns – confirmed it.

When the game was on the line in the fourth quarter, McCarthy abandoned the run and turned to Rodgers.

"We put everything on his shoulders," McCarthy said.

Pittsburgh had closed to within 21-17 when Rodgers led an eight-play drive that ended in an 8-yard touchdown pass to Greg Jennings. After the Steelers cut the lead to 28-25 with 7½ minutes left in the fourth quarter, Rodgers led an 10-play, 70-yard drive that ran 5½ minutes off the clock and set up Mason Crosby for an easy 23-yard field goal.

This championship also was about Rodgers taking his place next to Bart Starr and Brett Favre as great quarterbacks who led the Packers to Super Bowl wins. Starr was named MVP twice, in Super Bowls I and II. Rodgers now has his. Favre never won the award.

And as it had all season, the Packers' defense came through with big plays.

Safety Nick Collins returned an interception 37 yards for a touchdown and a 14-0 first-quarter lead. A second-quarter interception by backup cornerback Jarrett Bush set up the Packers' third touchdown. A fumble forced by linebacker Clay Matthews and recovered by linebacker Desmond Bishop stopped the Steelers in their tracks early in the fourth quarter and turned the momentum back to the Packers.

There wasn't a wild celebration in Green Bay's locker room after the game. Instead, in keeping with the character of this team, there were huge smiles, hugs and knowing nods.

It's as if these players knew they were capable of greatness. Now the rest of the world knows, too. ■

OPPOSITE: Green Bay Packers coach Mike McCarthy, second from right, holds the Vince Lombardi Trophy after winning Super Bowl XLV. Also on the podium are, from left, Packers president and CEO Mark Murphy, Fox broadcaster Terry Bradshaw and Packers general manager Ted Thompson. COREY WILSON/PRESS-GAZETTE

ABOVE: A Packers fan wears an old helmet and green-and-gold beads outside Cowboys Stadium before the game. JIM MATTHEWS/PRESS-GAZETTE

ABOVE RIGHT: Packers fans tailgate outside Lambeau Field in Green Bay before the game, setting up a living room and television. MATTHEW L. BECKER

RIGHT: A Packers fan takes a photo outside Cowboys Stadium before the game. JIM MATTHEWS/PRESS-GAZETTE

OPPOSITE: The Packers run onto the field after they were introduced as a team before the game. JIM MATTHEWS/PRESS-GAZETTE

LEFT: Safety Nick Collins (36) celebrates his 37-yard interception return for a touchdown during the first quarter with linebacker Clay Matthews. EVAN SIEGLE/PRESS-GAZETTE

OPPOSITE LEFT: Wide receiver Jordy Nelson hauls in a 29-yard touchdown pass against Steelers cornerback William Gay during the first quarter. EVAN SIEGLE/PRESS-GAZETTE

OPPOSITE RIGHT TOP: Quarterback Aaron Rodgers (12) cheers as wide receivers Greg Jennings (85) and Jordy Nelson, (87) celebrate Nelson's touchdown catch. COREY WILSON/PRESS-GAZETTE

OPPOSITE RIGHT BOTTOM: Safety Nick Collins returns an interception 37 yards for a touchdown during the first quarter. EVAN SIEGLE/PRESS-GAZETTE

ABOVE: Linebacker A.J. Hawk (50) calls a play in the defensive huddle during he second quarter. Facing him, from left, are linebacker Clay Matthews, cornerback Tramon Williams, defensive end Cullen Jenkins, cornerback Charles Woodson, linebacker Frank Zombo and cornerback Sam Shields. EVAN SIEGLE/PRESS-GAZETTE

RIGHT: Cornerback Jarrett Bush, center, reacts after intercepting a pass during the second quarter. He's flanked by linebacker Frank Zombo (58) and defensive end Cullen Jenkins (77). COREY WILSON/PRESS-GAZETTE

FAR RIGHT: Bush, left, celebrates his interception with linebacker Matt Wilhelm. EVAN SIEGLE/PRESS-GAZETTE

RIGHT: From left, safety Nick Collins, linebacker Frank Zombo and cornerbacks Sam Shields and Charles Woodson celebrate Collins' third-down stop of Steelers receiver Mike Wallace during the second quarter. COREY WILSON/PRESS-GAZETTE

FAR RIGHT: Steelers wide receiver Antwaan Randle El makes a leaping catch against cornerback Sam Shields during the second quarter. EVAN SIEGLE/PRESS-GAZETTE

BELOW RIGHT: Safety Nick Collins tackles against Steelers wide receiver Mike Wallace. EVAN SIEGLE/PRESS-GAZETTE

BELOW: Running back James Starks bursts through a hole during the second quarter. Steelers linebacker James Farrior is blocked at left. EVAN SIEGLE/PRESS-GAZETTE

ABOVE: Linebacker Frank Zombo sacks Steelers quarterback Ben Roethlisberger during the third quarter. It was the Packers' only sack of the game. EVAN SIEGLE/PRESS-GAZETTE

ABOVE LEFT: Quarterback Aaron Rodgers is sacked by Steelers linebacker LaMarr Woodley (56) during the third quarter. Steelers defensive end Ziggy Hood (96) closes in. COREY WILSON/PRESS-GAZETTE

LEFT: Steelers running back Rashard Mendenhall tumbles over cornerback Pat Lee on an 8-yard touchdown run during the third quarter. EVAN SIEGLE/PRESS-GAZETTE

OPPOSITE LEFT TOP: Wide receiver Greg Jennings scores on a 21-yard touchdown pass against Steelers safety Troy Polamalu (43) during the second quarter. COREY WILSON/PRESS-GAZETTE

OPPOSITE LEFT BOTTOM: Quarterback Aaron Rodgers celebrates his second-quarter touchdown pass to Jennings. EVAN SIEGLE/PRESS-GAZETTE

OPPOSITE RIGHT TOP: Jennings is lifted by center Scott Wells after his second-quarter touchdown catch. Running back James Starks (44) is at left. COREY WILSON/PRESS-GAZETTE

OPPOSITE RIGHT BOTTOM: Cornerback Charles Woodson winces after breaking his collarbone during the second quarter. He did not return to the game. EVAN SIEGLE/PRESS-GAZETTE

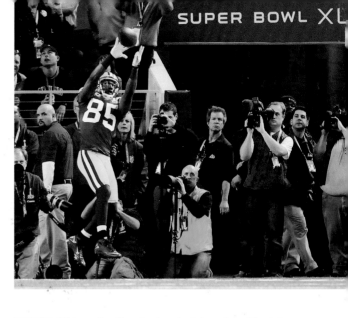

OPPOSITE: The offense huddles as quarterback Aaron Rodgers (12) calls a play. From left, the Packers players include running back James Starks (44), tackle Chad Clifton (76), wide receivers Greg Jennings (85) and Brett Swain (16), center Scott Wells (63), wide receivers James Jones (89) and Jordy Nelson (87) and tackle Bryan Bulaga (75). EVAN SIEGLE/PRESS-GAZETTE

LEFT: Linebacker Desmond Bishop, center, scoops up a fumble by Steelers running back Rashard Mendenhall during the fourth quarter. Behind him, from left, are Steelers tackle Ramon Foster, linebacker A.J. Hawk and safety Nick Collins. EVAN SIEGLE/PRESS-GAZETTE

BELOW: Bishop (55) celebrates with cornerback Tramon Williams after recovering the Mendenhall fumble. Defensive end Howard Green (95) and cornerback Jarrett Bush (24) are at left. EVAN SIEGLE/PRESS-GAZETTE

ABOVE: Wide receiver Greg Jennings hauls in an 8-yard touchdown pass during the fourth quarter. COREY WILSON/PRESS-GAZETTE

BELOW: Quarterback Aaron Rodgers celebrates after throwing one of two touchdown passes to Jennings. EVAN SIEGLE/PRESS-GAZETTE

ABOVE: Linebacker Desmond Bishop, left, and safety Nick Collins, right, try to contain Steelers wide receiver Mike Wallace during the fourth quarter. Cornerback Sam Shields is on the ground behind Wallace. COREY WILSON/PRESS-GAZETTE

ABOVE: Packers fans celebrate Greg Jennings' 8-yard touchdown catch during the fourth quarter. COREY WILSON/PRESS-GAZETTE

ABOVE LEFT: Cornerback Sam Shields, left, and safety Nick Collins, center, can't stop Steelers receiver Mike Wallace on a 25-yard touchdown catch during the fourth quarter. COREY WILSON/PRESS-GAZETTE

LEFT: Linebacker Desmond Bishop tackles Steelers tight end Heath Miller during the fourth quarter. COREY WILSON/PRESS-GAZETTE

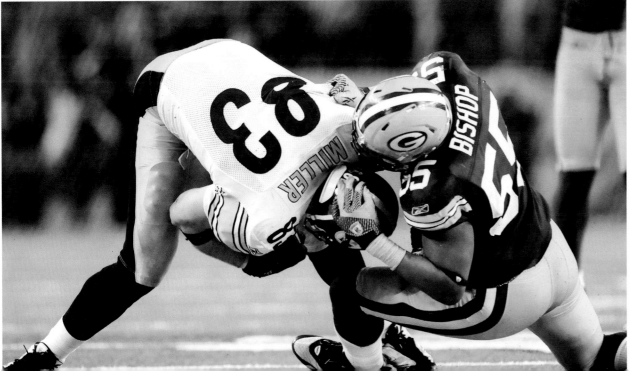

LEFT: Steelers defensive end Ziggy Hood flexes after making a stop during the fourth quarter. COREY WILSON/PRESS-GAZETTE

FAR LEFT: Wide receiver Jordy Nelson sprints between Steelers safety Ryan Clark (25) and linebacker James Harrison (92) after making a catch during the fourth quarter. EVAN SIEGLE/PRESS-GAZETTE

ABOVE: Cornerback Jarrett Bush hits Steelers quarterback Ben Roethlisberger, forcing an incomplete pass. EVAN SIEGLE/PRESS-GAZETTE

OPPOSITE: Wide receiver Greg Jennings cuts between Steelers cornerback Ike Taylor (24) and safety Troy Polamalu (43) after making a catch in the fourth quarter. EVAN SIEGLE/PRESS-GAZETTE

LEFT: Jennings reacts after making a catch during the fourth quarter. Steelers cornerback Ike Taylor is at left. EVAN SIEGLE/PRESS-GAZETTE

BELOW: The Packers' sideline celebrates after the defense stopped the Steelers on fourth down to clinch the victory in Super Bowl XLV. Cornerback Brandon Underwood (28), who was inactive, holds his hands to his head. EVAN SIEGLE/PRESS-GAZETTE

ABOVE: Quarterback Aaron Rodgers celebrates and points to the crowd as he leaves the field after the game. COREY WILSON/PRESS-GAZETTE

LEFT: Wide receiver James Jones is overcome with emotion as he kneels on the sideline after the game. EVAN SIEGLE/PRESS-GAZETTE

BOTTOM LEFT: Nose tackle B.J. Raji gets a hug from his father, Busari Raji Sr., after the game. EVAN SIEGLE/PRESS-GAZETTE

BOTTOM RIGHT: Linebacker A.J. Hawk (50) celebrates with safeties coach Darren Perry after the game. EVAN SIEGLE/PRESS-GAZETTE

ABOVE: Packers president emeritus Bob Harlan smiles as he watches the postgame festivities. He hired general manager Ted Thompson, who built a Super Bowl winner. COREY WILSON/PRESS-GAZETTE

ABOVE LEFT: Linebacker Clay Matthews, left, points to quarterback Aaron Rodgers after giving him a championship belt on the podium. COREY WILSON/PRESS-GAZETTE

LEFT: Safety Nick Collins holds up a championship towel. COREY WILSON/PRESS-GAZETTE

BELOW: Green-and-gold fireworks exploded over the Ray Nitschke Bridge in downtown Green Bay after the game. Thousands of people gathered downtown to celebrate the Packers' victory. MATTHEW L. BECKER

RIGHT: Cornerback Charles Woodson carries the Vince Lombardi Trophy as he walks around the field after the game. Woodson missed the second half with a broken collarbone. EVAN SIEGLE/PRESS-GAZETTE

BOTTOM LEFT: A Packers fan holds up the Green Bay Press-Gazette's extra section while he celebrates on Washington Street in downtown Green Bay after the game. MATTHEW L. BECKER

BOTTOM RIGHT: A homemade Vince Lombardi Trophy is held aloft as Packers fans celebrate on Washington Street in downtown Green Bay after the game. MATTHEW L. BECKER

2.7.11
WWW.PACKERSNEWS.COM
GREEN BAY **PRESS-GAZETTE**

PACKERS FINAL

G 31 25 » Packers win their fourth Super Bowl

TOUGH ENOUGH

Defense stops Steelers; Rodgers MVP

Fan shots

We asked readers to share their best Packers photos and the response was amazing! We received than 350 photos. Here are some of our favorites.

1: We're enjoying the pregame action on the field. (PHOTO BY SUE WISNESKI) **2:** The Hall family tailgating before the Dec. 26 Giants game and wearing the Aaron Rodgers belts. (PHOTO BY BRIAN SCHAEFER) **3:** Madeline Gagne and Katherine Carter enjoy a preseason game at Lambeau Field. (PHOTO BY KATHERINE CARTER) **4:** We met at Lambeau! (PHOTO BY CORINNE WESTPHAL) **5:** Tailgate. (PHOTO BY TRAVIS COOK) **6:** Group of Bay Port High School teachers making an annual road trip to a Packers away game: Kelly Fitzgerald, Mark Hebert, Mike Simoens and Harvey Knutson. (PHOTO BY KELLY FITZGERALD) **7:** We won! Bruce and Aggie Campbell. (PHOTO BY JIM OUDENHOVEN) **8:** Friends enjoying each other, the atmosphere and the Bear hunt! (PHOTO BY TYLER SMITH)

1: Packers fans. (PHOTO BY CARMEN GREENWOOD) **2:** Me showing my Packers spirit. (PHOTO BY KEVIN NETT) **3:** The guy who made me being at the game possible. Thanks for the once-in-a-lifetime seats! (PHOTO BY JASON CHILDERS) **4:** Enjoying the Atlanta playoff win! (PHOTO BY JOE KLEIBER) **5:** Enjoying a warm November day at Lambeau. (PHOTO BY ANONYMOUS) **6:** Group outside the stadium. (PHOTO BY MARY LAUFER) **7:** Paris, the dog of Paula Grassell, is a doggone good Packers fan in Seattle. (PHOTO BY DONALD L GRASSELL) **8:** Green-and-gold steak kabobs in Green Bay on Dec. 26. (PHOTO BY SAMANTHA MEDINGER)

1: Clay Zimmerman and Debbie Peserik tailgating before the Packers-Giants game. (PHOTO BY DEBBIE PESERIK) **2:** Gabriella, born Aug. 23, 2010, just in time to kick off the Packers' glorious 2010 season. (PHOTO BY AMANDA LYNN) **3:** Michael, Kathleen and Stephen. (PHOTO BY CORINNE WESTPHAL) **4:** Buffalo Bills fans from Forestville, N.Y., tailgating with us at Lambeaiu Field before Packers-Bills game on Sept. 19. From left, Pat and Charlie Zoerb and Rita and Jim Oudenhoven. The Zoerbs presented us with a Bills cutting board which Charlie made from a tree on his land in New York. (PHOTO BY JIM OUDENHOVEN) **5:** Packers fans. (PHOTO BY CARMEN GREENWOOD) **6:** God bless America and the Green Bay Packers. (PHOTO BY SHARON DRAKE) **7:** Joe and Tim. (PHOTO BY SHORTY LANDWEHR) **8:** Brady and Shannon Peserik met up with Santa, who gifted the entire Packers nation with a win over the New York Giants! (PHOTO BY DEBBIE PESERIK) **9:** A fantastic day at Lambeau, hanging out with all the best fans on Earth! (PHOTO BY CHARITY RAMER) **10:** Sisters Mary Wescott, Maureen Campbell and Kathy Hanke get a chance to watch a game together. (PHOTO BY KEN CAMPBELL) **11:** Aggie and Bruce Campbell. (PHOTO BY BRUCE CAMPBELL)

1: Tom, Peggy and Sam at the Dec. 26 Giants game. (PHOTO BY PEGGY HUBBLE) **2:** Packers fans. (PHOTO BY CARMEN GREENWOOD) **3:** The Erdmann family and friends tailgate. (PHOTO BY SARAH BERKEN) **4:** This photo was taken for the Packers Partners Club of Champions Group reception. I won having my picture taken with a few Packers players, along with some other Packers Partners Club of Champions members. I am the last man on the right side, top row. (PHOTO BY TERRY WALSH) **5:** Ready to watch the Eagles go down! (PHOTO BY TYLER SMITH) **6:** My brother and me. (PHOTO BY ALLISON PRAHL) **7:** Rick and Garrett Bloch's Super Bowl shrine. Something from each Super Bowl win. (PHOTO BY RICK BLOCH) **8:** Family and friends before the Packers-Falcons game. (PHOTO BY LOSSIE FIELDER) **9:** Brady Peserik reunited with some Packers fans he met at a previous game while watching the Packers beat his beloved New York Giants. (PHOTO BY DEBBIE PESERIK) **10:** This was the last practice our mom attended. She died of brain cancer on Sept. 8. She was a huge Packers fan and loved Aaron Rodgers! (PHOTO BY KATHERINE CARTER)

OUR PACKERS PHOTOGRAPHY TEAM (FRONT ROW FROM LEFT): **Evan Siegle, Jim Matthews, Corey Wilson.**

OUR PACKERS COVERAGE TEAM (BACK ROW FROM LEFT): **Kareem Copeland, Pete Dougherty, Mike Vandermause, Rob Demovsky.**

GREEN BAY PRESS-GAZETTE
greenbaypressgazette.com

PUBLISHER: **Kevin Corrado**

EXECUTIVE EDITOR: **John Dye**

RESEARCHER, EDITOR AND WRITER: **Jeff Ash**

ADDITIONAL WRITING: **Weston Hodkiewicz, Tony Walter**

ADDITIONAL PHOTOGRAPHY (GREEN BAY): **Matthew L. Becker, Michael P. King**

ADDITIONAL PHOTOGRAPHY (DETROIT): **Julian H. Gonzalez, Kirthmon F. Dozier, Detroit Free Press, used with permission**

BOOK DESIGN: **Chris Fenison, Pediment Publishing**